SAD TIGER

SAD TIGER

NEIGE SINNO

TRANSLATED BY
NATASHA LEHRER

SEVEN STORIES PRESS
NEW YORK · OAKLAND · LONDON

Originally published in 2023 by P.O.L Editeur, Paris, France.

This work received support from the French Ministry of Foreign Affairs and the Cultural Services of the French Embassy in the United States through their publishing assistance program.

SEVEN STORIES PRESS
140 Watts Street
New York, NY 10013
www.sevenstories.com

LIBRARY OF CONGRESS CATALOGING-IN-PUBLICATION DATA
is on file.

ISBN: 978-1-64421-552-4 (paperback)
ISBN: 978-1-64421-468-8 (ebook)

College professors and high school and middle school teachers may order free examination copies of Seven Stories Press titles. Visit https://www.sevenstories.com/pg/resources-academics or email academic@sevenstories.com.

Printed in India

9 8 7 6 5 4 3 2 1

CONTENTS

Chapter I—PORTRAITS

Chapter II—GHOSTS

It was something quite special,
that feeling: an oppressive, hideous
constraint, as if I were sitting with the
small ghost of somebody I had just killed.

—*Lolita*, Vladimir Nabokov

CHAPTER 1

PORTRAITS

Portrait of my rapist

Because for me too, when it comes down to it, the thing that's most interesting is what's going on in the perpetrator's head. With victims it's easy, we can all put ourselves in their shoes. Even if you've not experienced it, the traumatic amnesia, the bewilderment, the silence of the victim is something we can all imagine, or think we can.

The perpetrator, on the other hand, is a different story. Being in a room alone with a seven-year-old child, getting an erection from imagining what's about to happen. Saying the words to make the child come closer, putting the erection in the child's mouth, coaxing the child to open wide. That is fascinating. It's beyond comprehension. And after it's over getting dressed, going back to family life as if nothing has happened. And once the madness has taken hold, doing it again, doing it again and again, for years. Never telling a soul. Truly believing there will never be a denunciation, despite the steadily intensifying sexual abuse. Knowing there will never be a denunciation. And then one day when there is a denunciation, daring to lie, or daring to tell the truth, daring to admit it straight off. Still believing, after being sentenced to several years in prison, that the punishment is unjust. Proclaiming the right to be pardoned. Insisting this is a man, not a monster. And then, after being released from prison, making a fresh start.

I have seen this up close, as close as it is possible to see it, I have turned this question over in my mind for years, and still I do not understand.

The portrait

If you were to notice only one thing about him, it would be his energy. He is a man who is full of life. He is always moving, he's all action. He's been like that ever since he was little. His brothers too. Three boys, close in age, making mayhem in the small apartment in a Parisian banlieue. The father trying to concentrate on his painting, yelling that he can't work with all the noise. The mother trying to get the children to quiet down, taking them into another room or off to the park to let off steam, even when it was raining or windy. The father couldn't make a living as a painter, his real vocation, and so alongside the drawing classes he gave he set up a little business selling contemporary chimneypieces. It was the 1970s and 80s, nowadays his chimneypieces would look completely absurd or hilarious, depending on your point of view, in any case it wouldn't occur to anyone today to install one of his bizarre, psychedelic capsules with an integrated glass firebox in their living room. I think at the time, though, the business was quite successful. The grandparents on both sides were working class, from the North, around Boulogne-sur-Mer where the family still owned an apartment that they stayed in during vacations. The mother was, I think, the secretary for the business, a bit of a housewife, a bit in her husband's shadow. Nothing special, not rich, not poor, lower-middle-class Parisians. None of the children went to university, they left home before finishing high school. The eldest became a salesman, the second went into the army, and my stepfather left the city to do his military training in the Alps. He never returned to Paris. The parents were quite strict and old-fashioned in the way they brought up their children, with rules and discipline. He was proud of his tough upbringing, and of his time in the scouts, like he was about everything to do with his education. It had all contributed to developing his strength and his desire to live, discover, conquer.

I have a hard time imagining him living in the Parisian suburbs. I only ever saw him in the mountains, in sports gear or work overalls. Back then though he must have looked like a miniature office worker, going off to his Catholic school in an ironed shirt, polished shoes, hair plastered to his skull, until he was eighteen. That was when he left home for Briançon, where he discovered the mountains, climbing, paragliding, a life that was free and untrammeled, that didn't require him to wear a shirt, wait for the metro, comb his hair with a side part, or go to mass on Sunday. A life of fresh air and sunlight.

In 1983, the year he met my mother, he was twenty-four. They were on a course together, training to become mountain guides. He was tall, athletic, personable. He liked taking charge in the group, calling the shots in an emergency, in a tricky situation, on a dangerous bluff, if there was an accident. He was charismatic, had lots of friends, was attractive to girls.

He was attractive to her. He reminded her of the boyfriend who had been killed in an avalanche a few months before. She had been devastated by his sudden, shocking death. She thought she would never get over it. But perhaps, in fact, she would. She spent a lot of time with this new man. She liked his resolute nature. She liked that he was purposeful and cheerful. It was refreshing after Sammy, the father of her daughters, who was dreamy, odd, a little withdrawn. He quickly set about trying to win her over. He led her up steep paths to peaks where they gazed, mesmerized, at the beauty of the landscape. They walked in the mountains, in silence, one behind the other, beneath the ever-changing summer skies, clouds that moved like the flats of a theater set, appearing to slide toward the west to make way for other skies concealed beneath. They held hands as they walked back down. He was already with someone; she was four years older than him and had two small children. Two little girls, aged six and four, with fairy-tale names, Neige, which means snow, and Rose, they were living with their papa, but she couldn't leave them with him for too long, they needed her, and she missed them. She was surprised when, just a few weeks into their passionate affair, he told her he wanted to carry on, told her to bring the girls, said he wanted to try to build something together. She was surprised but happy, she told herself how lucky she was.

She liked his muscular physique, the energy he gave off. Yes, energy, strength, I've said that already. He skied, climbed, enjoyed physical labor, liked to push himself as hard and as far as he could. Before becoming a guide, he had trained with the mountain infantry, an elite regiment for young people who loved the Alps. They had to run the Route des Traverses in the snow at dusk, climb up to mountain refuge huts carrying eighty kilos of rocks in a backpack, dig ditches on the Col de l'Échelle pass with small aluminum shovels until blisters formed on their frozen hands, things like that. He'd loved it. She was a pacifist, she didn't understand what he liked about this world of arbitrary rules and demonstrations of masculinity. Especially after Sammy, with his horror of guns, uniforms and violence, who'd pretended to be mentally ill to avoid military service. But he told her about long hikes with his friends, the camaraderie they developed during these physical challenges, the hard-won lessons learned when facing the elements. Before all that, he'd always thought he was trapped in his gray banlieue. It was his love of the outdoors that led him to discover all these new things. Now he knew he would never leave, he had found his way in life, in nature, with her.

The mountains, the army, the banlieue. I've said all that already too.

She loved his face, with its high cheekbones and dark, almond-shaped eyes that suggested Asian ancestry floating in his otherwise Nordic features, this Frenchman from the north, the Pas-de-Calais, where his parents were from, pale skin, aquiline nose.

He dreamed of having a large family. It wasn't long

before he and my mother had two children of their own, a boy and then a girl. Whenever he was asked, he said he'd like to have eight children. People never knew what to say to that. They tried to hide their discomfiture. What they were really thinking was that four was already too many for them to cope with.

He never lost his taste for the butter and dairy of the land of his childhood. His mother used to make a kind of Yule log with buttercream and coffee, and for years, Christmas after Christmas, we tried, in vain, to reproduce it. It was never as good. Sometimes it was disgusting, with minuscule particles of butter that refused to melt studding the cream with horrid, fatty little pimples, and sugar that was gritty between the teeth. Sometimes the flavor and texture were almost as good as the original, and then our eyes hung on his face to interpret the final judgment, which transmitted a feeling of contagious happiness. It was as happy as we ever got as a family.

He burned in the sun and was violently allergic to pollen in the springtime. He sneezed like a lunatic.

He liked board games but was so short-tempered they always ended badly. Family sessions of Monopoly or games of strategy with friends often finished with a meltdown; he would suddenly stop playing in the middle of the game, slamming his fist on the table and sending all the little plastic pieces flying, the red hotels and the green houses, the pile of banknotes, and then he would storm out in a fury, banging the door behind him.

It was the same when he played tennis. How many times I saw him slam his racket on the ground. A racket is expensive, and we didn't really have the money to spend on something like that. But he couldn't help himself. He hurled insults at his opponent, at himself, at the ball that had landed outside the line. Red and sweaty, eyes glistening with rage, he stamped his foot and sent his racket flying into the net.

Okay, that's enough. I tried. I wanted to create a portrait from my perspective, today, that of an adult woman who is a mother. I wanted to try and see what my mother saw back then, what our friends saw, what people see in a body or a face, what you see when you read a description with the eyes of an adult who's used to decoding, who's used to descriptions of characters in novels or on the news, who's used to looking at and deciphering images. I can't do it. I've written a lot of stories and a few novels—surely I should be able to describe someone. But it's not the same. Firstly because I'm trying to stick to some hypothetical objective truth that I can't grasp, despite the photos and lingering memories. And then of course, it's impossible because it's him.

All right then, the portrait

He is tall and strong. Brutish, even. His voice switches smoothly from gentle to harsh. As soon as something irritates him, he shouts. Loudly. He thinks the way my sister and I have been brought up is completely abnormal, excessively permissive, indulgent. We've been turned into two little savages. It's a disgrace.

His hands are large, they often flush pinky-red, like his face when it's exposed to the sun or to anger. His hands are strong. They grip and caress, but with a kind of roughness, a caress that claims ownership, insistent. Like his voice, which tries too hard to sound soft, going up at the end of a sentence with a little note of questioning as if seeking his interlocutor's approval, confirmation that you agree with him, you're listening, you're willing. Except the tone doesn't change if you don't give your approval, if you stay silent or say no. The voice stays the same. In fact, this little note of uncertainty is part of his endlessly repeated monologue.

He is tall. His feet are ugly, like all feet, but uglier because they are hairy and pink and gnarled. It's odd that he has hairs on his feet because the rest of his body, his torso and arms, is smooth. It's his skin that's really ugly, mottled pink and white and red and brown. The skin of his penis, when it's taut over his erection, is purplish blue, then peachy-pink further from the glans, then beige and wrinkled on the testicles that dangle like a flap of dead skin or a bit of a corpse beneath the enormous penis rigid and hard as a bone.

I never once saw him holding a book, but he liked comics, especially ones set in the American Far West. He had almost the full collection of a comic series with a hero called Blueberry. He spent a long time reading them on the toilet. I was going to say he locked himself in the bathroom, but that's not true. When we eventually got a bathroom in the house it had no bolt on the door, nor did any of the bedrooms. He didn't want us to have any control over our privacy. Which, when I think about it now, seems a bit odd, it would have been convenient for him to be able to lock the door when he was alone in a room with me.

He adored Johnny Hallyday. And that meant we were all forced to listen to Johnny too, for hours on end, during long days spent working on the house, during family car journeys or late-night sessions with friends. The more we listened to the same songs, the more the lyrics began to seem to me seared with deep hypocrisy. All that drama about the decent man with a pure heart, the tough guy who is, deep down, a softy, the suffering macho man, that whole symphony of self-pity repulsed me.

My stepfather certainly thought of himself as a lonesome cowboy. He was always going on about his acute sense of injustice. There were a couple of anecdotes he liked to tell, about rough justice he'd witnessed in elementary school, how horrified he'd been. Whenever he caught my sister and me getting up to some mischief, he reprimanded the two of us severely, insisting on appropriate punishment. He would make us push wheelbarrows loaded with rocks from one end of the garden to the other, or dig holes or fetch wood.

He had high moral standards which we were never allowed to breach. I saw him several times when I was a child heroically going to someone's aid, in the mountains, at the scene of an accident or a fire. He worked for a few years as an ambulance driver. He oversaw safety and security on a team that worked on hazardous construction sites. He was transformed doing this kind of thing. He put his entire self into serving his objective, straining his muscles and his mind, almost aglow from within; people were always ready to follow his instructions, trusting his judgment and his instincts. He was the guide who led people to safety, the man who was prepared to sacrifice himself for the common good, who never wavered, even for a second, in the face of danger, fire, or snow. The embodiment of bravery.

For years I thought of him as godlike, larger than life. He seemed like a mythological creature, a Sisyphus, a Prometheus, tortured by demons. In retrospect, years later, I wonder if perhaps he was just a bit of a loser who had the gift of manipulating people and exploiting the vulnerability of someone more helpless than he. But within the shuttered world of our family, he was all-powerful. I guess he was both, a Titan and a loser. Who wouldn't rather see themselves as the victim of a Titan rather than a loser?

We did a lot of manual labor together. Mostly in the house, which we restored entirely ourselves, him, my mother, my sister, and me. My sister and I were little: We were given tasks to suit our size, transporting materials from one place to another, sanding walls, fetching tools for the grown-ups. We were like them, every weekend in the middle of the construction site in our frayed overalls spattered with cement. We shared the responsibility and satisfaction of physical work, hunger deliciously satisfied by a well-deserved sandwich when we took a break, the silent rumination as we concentrated on a precise gesture. All while listening to the radio or cassette tapes of John-ny's songs. Even today, whenever I hear one of his songs, and I often do because they are still enormously popular, it's difficult not to feel the blade of a knife reopening a wound, as if the lyrics have a hidden meaning, always the same one, that only I can hear.

When your mouth goes all soft
When your body goes hard
When the sky in your eyes
Is suddenly no longer pure,
When your hands are willing
When your fingers don't dare
When your modesty says no
In a tiny, soft voice
I love you so, I love you so, I love you so

He said he loved me. He said he made me do what he made me do to show his love, he said his dearest wish was for me to love him back. He said the reason he started being like that with me, touching me, stroking me, was because he needed to be closer to me, because I refused to be sweet, because I would never say I loved him. Sometimes he punished me for my indifference to him by raping me. He promised me that if I didn't tell anyone he wouldn't touch the other children. Later, he said that if I told him I loved him, if I acted as if I loved him, he would change his behavior. I couldn't. It was too late, it was impossible now, I would rather have died than say those words to him. He said he would stop on the condition I be nice to him, at least in front of other people. I said yes. That's how it stopped.

The tip of the tongue taking a trip of three steps

I'm rereading *Lolita* by Vladimir Nabokov. The first time I read it was for an American literature class on transgressive writers that included Henry Miller, William Burroughs, and Charles Bukowski. I was twenty, drawn to the topic by the extreme experiences, the self-destruction and madness, but reading *Lolita* threw me off. I wasn't expecting to find so much overlap with my own grim history.

What makes the book so provocative, even more than the story itself, is the perspective through which it is told. The fact that the narrator is the guilty party, the pedophile, and the reader is obliged, through his voice, to enter his thoughts, to penetrate the mysteries of his reasoning, his justifications, his fantasies, is what makes the book so fascinating and troubling. The reader goes from acceptance to rejection, from disgust to compassion, from smiling at the narrator's strange sense of humor to sheer horror. We understand him and we don't understand him, we follow his madness to the bitter end, we dread his victories and rejoice at his fall from grace. This choice of perspective gives the pact between reader and writer a sophisticated subtlety: We play along with the author, imagining ourselves in the criminal's shoes, without remotely feeling empathy for him. And if ever we do allow ourselves to get carried away, at certain moments the text reminds us that our empathy with this monster makes us complicit.

It's an unusual choice. There are plenty of novels written from the victim's point of view, but few that identify with the perpetrator, and certainly not in the realist genre. Or to be more specific: It's an unusual choice when the subject is child rape. When it comes to other crimes, the reader might well be on the side of the criminal. We willingly imagine the thief, the traitor, even the murderer. The taboo in our culture is not rape itself, which is commonplace everywhere, it is talking about it, thinking about it, analyzing it.

My stepfather never once uttered the word rape. Even in front of the jury that found him guilty of that very crime he insisted it was something else.

The first chapters of *Lolita* are a deep dive into the mind of Humbert Humbert and his vision of the little girl as a seductive nymphet. She seems, he claims, genuinely to become his partner, they have a real bond, the two of them allied against her mother who tries to put up barriers against their relationship. Lolita is interested in things that aren't typical for her age, actresses in glamour magazines, Hollywood romances. She seeks the attention of the man who has seduced her mother and is thrilled when she gets it. She goes to see him in his office, sits by him on the couch, lays her naked legs nonchalantly in his lap. (Just being in the same house as him, bumping into him in the bathroom, in that little body, those clothes, with that smile, or absence of a smile, is provocative.) She wants something from him. And he thinks he knows what it is, because it's what he wants too. (There was the same framing of consent in my stepfather's words. You like that, don't you? You like that, yes, yes you do, you really like it.) He repeats it, tries to convince himself, but there's always a hint of doubt, because he knows deep down she does not want the same thing he does. It is precisely when he gets what he wants, when he passes from fantasy to the act itself, that the tone of the book changes. This is when the famous line appears about the small ghost, and the comedy turns to tragedy.

Most criminals invent stories that make it possible for them to live with themselves. Most perverts tell themselves that what they feel and do is rooted in love. (*You may jeer at me, and threaten to clear the court, but until I am gagged and half-throttled, I will shout my poor truth. I insist the world know how much I loved my Lolita. And then, I loved you. I was a pentapod monster, but I loved you. I was despicable and brutal, and turpid, and everything, mais je t'aimais, je t'aimais!)* The first chapters of *Lolita* are a fabulous demonstration of this kind of mental scaffolding. The skillful construction is so convincing, it almost makes the world that the predator invents seem real, and at the same time, thanks to a whole series of signs, the reader can tell that it is utterly delusional.

More than anything else, Humbert sees himself as a victim. Of bad luck, of other people, of himself. He is the plaything of his involuntary impulses. His obsession for nymphets comes from his unconscious, a moment of grace experienced in childhood that comes back to him in a way he can't control. He is the victim of a hypocritical society that pretends not to tolerate love between children and adults except when it comes to important men, for whom everything is permitted. *After all, Dante fell madly in love with his Beatrice when she was nine. . . . And when Petrarch fell madly in love with his Laureen, she was a fair-haired nymphet of twelve.*

If we were in a different place or a different time, we would be left alone to carry on our love affair. It's natural, and you can't fight nature. But in this world, no one understands. And that is why no one must know.

The other story he invents is about seduction. *I am going to tell you something very strange: it was she who seduced me.* It is obvious that he is exaggerating every last detail of Lolita's unlikely complicity. The novel is written in such a way that the reader is witness to a permanent double game of perverse consciousness that transforms aspects of reality in order to justify his fantasy. But many readers take the absurdity literally. They too visualize a debauched Lolita, attracted to her stepfather, playing at provocation, deliberately seeking him out.

You like that? Yes, yes you do, you really like it.

The title is *Lolita* but Lolita herself is almost entirely absent. You see her through the filter of her predator's gaze, and she almost never exists as herself; she is the perfect fantasy figure, the nymphet incarnate. At last, at the end of the book, Humbert the dreamer recognizes this. As he sits in the car he has deliberately driven off the road, waiting for the police to pick him up, he has a final epiphany. He recalls the morning when he was driving around the country trying to find the teenage runaway. Lost on a mountain road, he stopped the car. Looking down from the hill to a small town below, sounds floated up toward him like a choir: *I stood listening to that musical vibration from my lofty slope, to those flashes of separate cries with a kind of demure murmur for background, and then I knew that the hopelessly poignant thing was not Lolita's absence from my side, but the absence of her voice from that concord.*

There are various ways this might be interpreted. There is the small ghost from the beginning of the novel, his guilt at not having allowed Lolita the chance to be a child like any other. I also hear an admission of *the absence of her voice* from the novel in general. The few times she speaks, it is clear that what she feels and sees is quite different from what her stepfather claims. *"You chump,"* she said, smiling sweetly at me. *"You revolting creature. I was a daisy-fresh girl,* and look what you've done to me? I ought to call the police and tell them you raped me. Oh, you dirty, dirty old man." In most of the dialogue where she is quoted in direct speech, her words are a protest against the insistence of this man forcing himself on her. "Pulease, leave me alone, will you," you would say. "For Christ's sake, leave me alone."

No, I don't like it. I never liked it, not once.

Occasionally Humbert realizes. In the middle of some self-centered litany, like scoria emerging at the surface, the girl's voice reveals to him an interior world that he would prefer to be able to ignore.

> I recall certain moments, let us call them icebergs in paradise, when after having had my fill of her—after fabulous, insane exertions that left me limp and azure-barred—I would gather her in my arms with, at last, a mute moan of human tenderness (her skin glistening in the neon light coming from the paved court through the slits in the blind, her soot-black lashes matted, her grave gray eyes more vacant than ever—for all the world a little patient still in the confusion of a drug after a major operation)—and the tenderness would deepen to shame and despair, and I would lull and rock my lone light Lolita in my marble arms, and moan in her warm hair, and caress her at random and mutely ask her blessing, and at the peak of this human agonized selfless tenderness (with my soul actually hanging around her naked body and ready to repent), all at once, ironically, horribly, lust would swell again—and "oh, no," Lolita would say with a sigh to heaven, and the next moment the tenderness and the azure—all would be shattered.

We must hear the howl in this powerless *no*. If Humbert himself, who would prefer to remain deaf, can hear it, we have to be able to hear it too.

The reader that Nabokov envisages is intelligent, capable of discernment, able to turn against a despicable narrator and to resist falling into the trap of compassion. The book is what is known in literary criticism as a tour de force, a technical feat that enables the author if not to condemn the crime, at least to expose its monstrousness through the words of a narrator who appears to be extolling its virtues.

And yet there are serious readers, by which I mean people who dedicate their life to reading, no fools they, like Maurice Couturier, a Nabokov scholar and his principal translator into French, who, although he obviously condemns such acts in real life, has argued that *Lolita* is a story of love and desire, all the more consuming for being founded on a taboo. For the American novelist Mary Gaitskill, *Lolita* is about love, warped, twisted, demented, and cruel, but love all the same. How can it be? Something that is not mutual may be many things, but surely it cannot be love. In *Lolita*, Humbert is alone in what he feels. To love without being loved in return, to desire without being desired in return, to dispense caresses without consent—how can that be a love story? The narrator is, from beginning to end, alone with his desire, his obsession, his compulsion. He is accompanied only by his fantasy, and then by Lolita's ghost. When he is with her, he cannot but notice that she does not follow him, she never consents, *never did she vibrate under my touch*. He knows that she will end up escaping him. He watches her as much as he can. He knows she wants to leave. And when she does, she has no choice but to use the exit offered her by another depraved man.

Why then has the book's cover, ever since the 1950s, so often carried an image of a lascivious, provocative adolescent, clearly older than the Lolita in the novel, who is only twelve when her rapist draws her into his long journey to perdition? Did Nabokov write an ambiguous novel, in which one might believe the girl to be a willing participant in the relationship? I don't think so: It's so obvious that she is not. There is a sensuality in the young girl's character as she is beginning to discover the world, yearning to rebel against her mother's strict rules, but the novel is, fundamentally, from the first time he acts on his desire to when she runs away, a story of manipulation and coercion.

One might suppose that *Lolita*'s reception took its author by surprise, for he could hardly have planned to create the quintessential image of the seductive nymphet in the popular imagination, even though in France it first came out with a publisher specializing in erotic texts. I can imagine doing the same thing if I'd written a masterpiece that was rejected by every respectable publishing house, telling myself there would be plenty of time to set the record straight. Twenty-five years later, in 1975, Nabokov appeared on the French literary television show *Apostrophes*, to set the record straight: Lolita is not a "slightly perverse little girl," but "a poor child who has been corrupted." It is quite possible that he was unaware how widespread the sexualization of children is and always has been. Maybe he was unaware of the sexual exploitation of children within the family, at school, in the Church, so incredibly common yet always talked about as if it were an aberration, an exceptionally rare and monstrous phenomenon. Or maybe he did know; maybe he deliberately built his fame on this scandalous ambiguity.

I still love the novel. Though it disturbs me deeply, I like the game of entering into the mind of someone who is deliberately immoral, who knows he is destroying another person, yet who nonetheless keeps doing it. He is caught in an infernal spiral, subjugated and humiliated by his impulses, by what he has become capable of feeling and doing. It is a whirlwind of sensation and thought, a fabulous antidote to the tedium of the modern world. Even humiliation, punishment and jail become an adventure for him, the culmination of a project that he himself devised and brought to fruition, obviously with unpredictable risks, but largely according to his own desires. He becomes the demiurge of his own life, and we are exhilarated by it too, though we regret it afterward, because we must, for that is the price we must pay for what Nabokov called aesthetic bliss.

A bedroom at dusk

My stepfather is a pervert too, but not a narcissistic and literary pervert like Humbert Humbert. He is a "narcissistic pervert with sadistic tendencies," if I recall correctly the term employed by the expert who undertook his psychiatric evaluation before the trial. The story he tells is not one of seduction, but a slightly more bizarre theory that he told himself so often he came firmly to believe it. He repeated it all through my childhood and during his cross-examination, as if his mental contortions had a kind of irrefutable logic, and everyone ought to be able to recognize the inevitability of what had led him to do what he had done.

When we first meet I am six and he is twenty-four. He comes into my life with the best intentions in the world. Humble but honest, he wants to replace my father, to love me like his own daughter, to give me a home, a stable family life, an education worthy of the name. I resist him from the start. I don't want to call him papa. I already have a papa. I don't need his love, his education, his hugs. I don't want him to touch me. I don't let him come near me. All he wants is for me to love him. He tries to get close to me. I push him away. So he comes at night and touches me, when I am not on the defensive. He realizes that in secret, in the dark, when he puts his fingers on my body and wakes me, muttering softly without pause, I don't dare push him away. I seem to understand that this is the only way for us to have an affectionate relation-ship. That's it: If I don't say anything at night, but during the day I am sullen and refuse to do anything he asks, it means there is no alternative.

Later, once it's started, once you've actually done it, *passé à l'acte*, it's too late, it's a thing. You should stop, you know you should. You promise yourself you'll stop. You stop for a few days, then it comes over you again. There's no barrier, and no one to help. You can't talk about it to anyone, it would be frowned upon, misunderstood, society is too closed, too intolerant. So you carry on, start up again, again and again, until the victim, years later, at last figures out a way to escape.

I remember places. The first place, a bedroom in darkness. I am woken by hands on me. Then his voice, when I open my eyes he is speaking in a low voice, he doesn't stop talking. I don't want to wake my sister asleep in bed beside me. I was seven when we lived in that apartment, I didn't understand what was happening, but from the first moment I sensed it was something serious and terrible. He was talking like a tamer speaks to a gentle but wild horse, a horse that needs to be held to stop it getting away. He was talking as if nothing in all this should scare me, and if I was scared it was fine, he was there, he would help me get over my fear. But he too was afraid, and the fear enveloped us like a layer of night.

Virginia Woolf, who was abused by her two half brothers, describes the bizarre experience of those first pawing caresses in an autobiographical piece in which she is trying to find a relationship between her old memories and the way her still-developing personality was being formed: . . . *as I sat there, he began to explore my body. I can remember the feel of his hand going under my clothes; going firmly steadily lower and lower. I remember how I hoped that he would stop; how I stiffened and wriggled as his hand approached my private parts. But it did not stop. His hand explored my private parts too.* Without calling it abuse, writing about it as simply one among several unpleasant experiences, she briefly analyzes, with a clarity notable for its candor and good sense, the emotions she felt, what would in the future come to be called traumatic shock:

I remember resenting, disliking it—what is the word for so dumb and mixed a feeling? It must have been strong, since I still recall it. This seems to show that a feeling about certain parts of the body; how they must not be touched; how it is wrong to allow them to be touched; must be instinctive.

It is a moment outside time, unbound from the course of history, so charged with absurdity and meaning that it eludes any attempt at narrative comprehension. I think it was the first time anyone ever touched me there, the first time I was lied to—and I knew without a shadow of a doubt that I was being lied to—the first time I found myself in this dark land with no idea which way to turn, my senses alert, the first time that my imperiled life, at its most intense yet to me seemingly so fragile, was revealed to me in its luminous singularity.

He has his good qualities too

I remember these words my mother came out with when we criticized him. We were so happy whenever he went away for a few days or weeks to work on a construction site. We discussed him, tried to analyze his temper, to figure out the exact moment of rupture that would lead to the explosion, so we could predict and thus avoid it. We concocted plans so things would be better when he came home. We cleaned the house obsessively so that it would be sparkling when he got back. I never said a word about the sexual abuse. But I furiously criticized everything else about him. His fixations, the arbitrary prohibitions he imposed on us all, his furious outbursts, his disapproval. My mother told us there was nothing we could do to change him, he would never change, it was up to us to make sure he was happy, and then he would leave us be. Like the almighty Minotaur, he had to be fed, cajoled, indulged, and only then might we hope he would not unleash his rage on us.

You have to remember his good qualities, my mother said.

The witnesses who testified on his behalf at the trial said that too. They couldn't insist that it was impossible for a man like him to have raped a child, since he had already confessed. If he hadn't, they certainly would have. Okay, so he'd done it, but other than that he was a great guy.

The far side of the moon is an abstract concept. It doesn't matter how many times we're told it's there, how many rational explanations we're given for why we cannot see it, it's virtually impossible to believe in. There is a definite logic to the explanation, but at the same time it is almost inconceivable. The moon rotates around the earth at exactly the same rate that it turns on its own axis, which means that it always shows the same side to our searching eyes. It seems so strange though. Why would it do that?

Human beings have always projected themselves onto the near side of the moon. In Mexico they see a rabbit. The image is perfectly clear.

Because we can never see it, we think the far side must be in darkness. But science refutes this notion. The sun's rays reach the far side just as they reach the near side. It too is lit up. Apparently it looks very different from the side we see from the earth. The visible side appears unfluctuating, smooth, made of flat rock; the side we can't see is cratered with clefts and ridges.

As far as most people are concerned it is in darkness. Darkness has nothing to do with light. The scientific explanation is not enough. The description is not enough. It's simply impossible to believe something so counterintuitive when you cannot see it.

Some of us were what's known today as neo-rurals, while others came not from the city but from other remote parts of the countryside. Either way, we were strangers to the village, people who didn't come from there. We lived a little outside the village, as is often the case for people who come from elsewhere. We rented apartments in houses left empty by their owners, who had moved away to Marseille or even Paris, and who came back only for vacations.

My mother, stepfather, and a few others created, out of necessity, a small community of sorts; what they all had in common was that they weren't from the village, they didn't live off the land, they were young, and they loved the mountains. They had similar lifestyles, worked in tourism and sports; spent winters in ski stations and summers on campsites, guiding walkers, taking tourists out on the river, up into the hills or down into the valleys; they worked as waiters in restaurants or making up beds in hotels. When they got older, they would retrain as health-care or construction workers, but for now they formed a contingent of irregular employees barely qualified to work in the leisure facilities run by a small oligarchy of locals who had inherited the land.

Some of these young people stayed for a few years

before going off to explore elsewhere. Others decided to settle here and bought up dilapidated farms on the edge of the village to restore. Which is what we did. My mother and stepfather, neither of them yet thirty, with the very modest earnings of seasonal workers with no qualifications, on the lowest rung of this small community of people working in rural tourism, borrowed money from their families and, at a very high interest rate, from the bank. As soon as the sale agreement was signed, they moved into what was an uninhabitable wreck and set up a makeshift camp, in the belief that the work would progress quickly, and we would soon have a bathroom, a kitchen, and the rest. But fixing up a ruin requires more than dreams and enthusiasm, and we lived in a construction site for the ten years it took me to graduate high school and leave home. At first the conditions were desperate. We lived in a damp basement with all our belongings heaped into piles that divided the space into different areas; after a while we moved upstairs into a large blue-and-white room whose lustrous tiles stood for a future in a gleaming house that would never be ours.

Our life was modest. We might have been described as poor, but it was a deliberate poverty, elected, almost, for it was their choice to live that way, a way of living in a place they chose to live, in touch with nature, in a home they owned. It was a poverty filled with dignity and hope. The inhabitants of the village didn't feel threatened by us, not like the neo-rurals of today, who only leave their home-working bubble to pick up groceries from the organic market, who raise the local cost of living, for whom the villagers are merely the folkloric background to their new environment. The locals looked at us with incredulous smiles, their only comment on our hippy hijinks a nod of the head or some sardonic expletive in the local dialect. They gave away eggs and milk for the children and were happy to lend out the corner of a field for us to have a vegetable patch and to plant potatoes.

There were no shops in the village, apart from a little hotel-restaurant, and a café-grocery store where fresh bread was delivered daily, situated on the side of the road near a small river from which it took its name, the Rif. The grocer knew the whole village and gave credit. Everyone paid their bill at the end of the month when they received their wages. We tried not to use the service too often, but during the second half of the month our mother invariably sent my sister and me to buy bread, pasta, and rice, and we had to ask nicely if it would be possible to have it on account. My mother never went on her own, presumably because she thought the woman would never refuse to give us children credit, and perhaps also because she felt ashamed. She must have thought we were too little to feel such a thing. But actually I remember very clearly the burning sadness and anger in my throat, the moment when we would have done anything not to have to utter the words of deliberate humiliation to obtain such a pathetic favor, so completely out of proportion to the immense effort it took to ask. I still feel it sometimes in situations where I have no reason to feel such unease, when I'm queuing in a government building for some paperwork for example. I remember the tiny, irritated hesitation in the grocer's voice that made it clear she might or might not agree to give us credit, the relief when she said yes, how we ran off straightaway with our groceries in a plastic bag, and the bitter feeling of power-lessness as we made our way back to the house.

Many years later, aged thirty and now living far from the village, I first read Annie Ernaux's books with the glowing sensation of listening to a voice shining a light on something inside me. I was surprised to discover that her parents used to run a little grocery store. People talk about Ernaux as someone who describes so perfectly the perception of betrayal experienced by so-called class defectors. I don't know what I was expecting, but it certainly wasn't that her parents had a store, even though it's a perfectly normal thing for working-class people to do. Because of my memories of the Rif, the experience of shame and discreet humiliation, I thought that grocers, who got to choose to give credit or not according to their whim, were bourgeois.

It's true there was something vulnerable about me, something profoundly solitary and alienated that predisposed me to being a victim. I knew that if he were arrested, we would be left with nothing, we would be destitute—it's not a complicated calculation, raising four children on the income of someone who cleans other people's homes for a living. That's without factoring in the disgrace, for of course everyone would know. He gave me the image of my mother as a fragile woman, kind of a misfit, incapable of surviving without him, completely dependent on him financially and emotionally. She probably was a bit. It was he who told me she had tried to commit suicide after her lover died in an avalanche when my sister and I were little. She wouldn't survive another calamity. What about me? Was I ready to inflict it on her? I cried a lot, especially when I was with him, at least he knew why I was crying, at least with him I could let go without anyone asking dangerous questions. He consoled me. Like Lolita, I was trapped. I didn't have anywhere else to go either.

At the hotel we had separate rooms, but in the middle of the night she came sobbing into mine, and we made it up very gently. You see, she had absolutely nowhere else to go.

Portrait of a nymphet

Was I pretty? I don't know. Like all rape survivors, I can't really position myself in terms of my physical appearance. But I'm not talking about today, I'm talking about when I was a child. I can make the effort to be objective and try to look at her as if she were someone else. I see in photos a girl with blond hair and big green eyes, a mischievous smile, hair all over the place, a bit wild. My daughter is ten. She looks like me. I must have looked quite like her, small for my age, skinny legs and arms, movements like a bird. With the right costume, I could have been a character out of a fairy tale, Alice in Wonderland, Little Red Riding Hood, Goldilocks, the Little Match Girl. Mind you, we know what happens to these girls, both too innocent and too brazen, who stick their noses where they don't belong.

I stayed skinny and bony for a long time. No breasts, no feminine shape, zero curves. I was late to puberty compared with my girlfriends. I got my first period when I was fourteen or fifteen. I was taciturn and shy, spent all my free time reading. I was a very good student, a bit too good, I was bored in class, I annoyed the others. I was made to skip a grade but it wasn't enough, I was still insolent at school, I stood up for myself and answered back. I was one of those kids who was never happy with a simple answer to a question, I was always shooting back, with a thirst to learn that my teachers found irritating. I wore secondhand clothes, corduroy overalls, flowery shirts, dresses that were too big, which I wore with ill-matched hiking shoes that gave my waiflike body a rather comical air. How could a child like that possibly attract the attention of a grown man? What does he see when he sees her? What could be erotic in a little scrap of a thing with scabby knees who still hasn't lost all her milk teeth, who's capable of spending an hour trying to catch lizards between the hot stones of the afternoon?

Innocence. That's what there is to see, the purest innocence. And perhaps what attracts him is simply the possibility of destroying it.

I remember a very bizarre situation with a family friend, a painter. I wasn't yet ten. We were on vacation in Boulogne-sur-Mer. He had painted my sister and me once before, a nice portrait he'd done when he came to visit us in the Alps. He wanted to paint me again. I remember being alone with him in his studio. I am wearing a little blue dress. I am sitting. He tells me to stand up. He turns back to the canvas, does a few quick sketches. He closes the door to the studio and tells me to take off my panties.

I remember it perfectly. Did it really happen? I remember becoming hard as a stone, saying to myself, it's not true, it's happening again. I don't know what happened then. I don't think he touched me, he just painted my portrait without panties.

I had to wear a corset when I was a teenager, with an ugly metal neck brace that I vaguely tried to hide under a bandana. I had acne, I gelled my hair into hideous styles, wore plastic earrings, jeans and T-shirts full of holes. And still men found me attractive. I think they sensed something defiant in me. I'd held onto a kind of pride from my untamed childhood that was reinforced by my unceasing revolt against the daily abuse. Does defiance provoke desire? I don't know. I remember the looks I got from some of the fathers whose families I babysat for, the glances from a few of my teachers. Did they read it in my features that I was doing it with another man, an adult the same age as they? Did they sense the possibility? Was I provoking them? Perhaps I was just trying to understand something. The thing that should have been obvious to them, to everyone, was my profound vulnerability. If anything were to happen to me, there was no one to save me. I think people can sense these things. And the opposite too: When you know you're protected, when you know people won't abandon you, you are not such easy prey. I am not sure about any of this, it's a flimsy hypothesis. But what I am sure about is the predatory atmosphere I often sensed around me. I always managed to get away the moment I noticed the look. Nothing ever happened. I never slept with any of them, apart from an instructor in charge of a group of teenagers at the youth activity center in the town where I was in junior high.

It happened during the end-of-year trip that had been months in the planning. I was fourteen, he was thirty-five. A current of sexual and romantic energy coursed through the group. There were ten of us, and when we got to Morocco we met up with other friends who were on vacation with their families. We hung out together, shared secrets and kisses. I was in love with one of the Moroccan boys, we held hands as we wandered around the souk. The instructor gave us a bit of freedom while keeping an eye on us. He let us explore our adolescent passion without getting into any kind of dangerous situation. He was a nice guy. We liked to tease him whenever he tried to change the music on the minibus. He loved Barbara and Francis Cabrel, and we wanted reggae or rap. I must have led him on a bit, or maybe he just wanted to feel like he was in on the game, one of the gang, even though he didn't belong. I remember gently resisting his advances. Then after a while I thought go on, you might as well do it, get it over with, then he'll leave you alone. Was that really how it happened? I'm not sure. For one thing, there was never any trial, which would have allowed him to describe what happened from his perspective. He had a narrow escape though. He said he was in love, crazy in love, he wanted to see me again. I told him, tersely, to stop, to leave me alone, that after the trip it was all over. He wanted to write to me. I point-blank refused. He wrote to me anyway. Obviously all the letters I was sent passed through other hands before reaching mine, and my stepfather found out about the affair. He was irate. He summoned me, in the presence of my mother (imagine, dear reader, the surreal scene that ensued, the three of us debating how both to protect and punish me, and above all how to punish my seducer), and we decided (he decided and my mother and I acquiesced) to threaten the instructor that we would report him to the police for "corrupting a minor" unless he promised never to contact me again for any reason and to immediately quit his job at the youth center. I wasn't at the meeting, but I'm sure my stepfather threatened him with all the aplomb he could muster, without an ounce of irony, considering the situation. Perhaps he thought he was justified in his mission to protect me from the depraved maneuvers of a dangerously corrupting influence. I felt terrible that the guy lost his job because of me. But he'd got himself into this mess. I'd told him not to write to me.

The first time we were alone after the business with the instructor from the youth center my stepfather laid into me. Why him and not me? Why did you reject me but you wanted it with another guy? He cried. He must have wanted me to do or say something to console him. I watched him cry and said nothing, felt nothing, neither compassion nor any sense of victory, nothing. I just waited for him to stop.

He read my mail, went through my things, controlled what I wore, who I saw, my social life, my girlfriends, my pocket money.

He never told me to do my homework, asked what we were studying in class, or showed any interest in the books I was reading.

I was given a lovely little notebook for my twelfth or thirteenth birthday, its cover inscribed with the words *Private Journal* in Gothic lettering. I decided this would be a good way to begin writing. I always knew writing was going to be the focus of my life. I began doing it without any ulterior motive, I didn't even want to record anything especially private in the notebook. But I kept it a little bit hidden between some books, so that the rest of the family wouldn't find it. I didn't think of this notebook as a secret, it was just my own space. A few weeks later he summoned me. He told me he had read every word, from beginning to end, and that one of these days this business with the journal might pose a risk for him. He also told me it would please him to be able to penetrate my mind even further through reading my journal. I was permitted to continue, but I had to promise not to write about us.

The following day I burned the notebook in the woodstove. Winter was over and we weren't making fires anymore, but I used the stove to hold the pages as they were consumed by the flames. I remember I set about it as a sort of ritual. I was bidding farewell that day, and for the rest of my life, to my journal, not only the one on those sheets of paper but the very concept of a private journal. I couldn't allow myself to create an object that made me so easily accessible, that might put me even more at the mercy of any person who wanted to spy on me or hurt me.

Dear reader, kindred spirit, sister, I have a confession to make, for I have no desire to mislead you: Beware my words, they will always be veiled. Don't ever imagine that this book is a confession. There is no private journal, no possibility of authenticity, no possibility of lies. My space does not exist inside this text, it only exists inside me.

Bizarre

As I read over these first pages, I realize I keep repeating the adjective *bizarre*. Bizarre experience, bizarre situation, bizarre explanation. It jumps off the page. Perhaps I should try and find a synonym to vary the style. I probably should. But this is a memoir, not a work of great literature, it's not meant to be polished, that would make it feel like a construction, would impact its authenticity. To be honest, I find the repetition eloquent, it expresses the mix of bewilderment and unease I feel when I think about this bizarre violence, the way often, in the case of domestic child sexual abuse, it takes on the appearance of a slow and tender act. I felt it at the time, and I feel it now as I try to put my memories down on paper. Everything to do with rape takes place in another dimension, a *bizarre* dimension, physically the same as the one in which the rest of life happens, superimposed onto it like a duplicate of unbearable clarity. People who survive car crashes talk about a similar kind of perception, everything is magnified, intensified, charged with energy, but at the same time the person is observing what's happening, unable to react, too slow, out of time, the tragedy is happening to us, to our body, but taking place outside us.

Sexual freedom

I guess it was the atmosphere of absurdity that allowed me to be convinced (not that I had the choice) by the things he said to me: What felt like a constraint was the very thing that would one day set me free, make me a liberated woman; I was never to tell anyone because even if I did no one would understand me; doing it would lead to desire; one day I'd find I was enjoying it. These reversals were the basis of our perverse logic.

He told me how difficult it had been for him getting to puberty without having had a minimum of sex education. He came from a prudish, religious family with a mother who was very present and a father who was very distant. The mother never told them anything about the body and its passions. He had this memory of appalling humiliation when his first girlfriend rejected him, he said, because of his ignorance and awkwardness about sex. He didn't want that to happen to me. And to be fair, that was one problem I didn't have.

He told me about contraception before I got my first period, taught me to kiss with my tongue, named, for my information, the parts of the body and positions. For when I'd have relationships with boys later on (even though the minute he found out about some minor flirtation he flew into a rage).

He told me that a sexual relationship between a child and an adult is disapproved of in our culture, even though in other societies it isn't a problem (he didn't have the cultural references to bring up Petrarch and Dante, but he had a pretty kinky take on sexuality in ancient Greece and various African and Native American tribes, not to mention great artists whose ideas were more sophisticated than those of the common people).

He showed me examples of precocious young girls. We didn't have a television at home, but one Christmas while we were staying with my maternal grandparents, we were watching some festive program with Vanessa Paradis in a miniskirt singing "Joe le taxi." She's almost the same age as you, he said innocently in front of the rest of the family, throwing me a meaningful look. I dressed like her all through junior high: black miniskirt and pantyhose, white shirt tucked into the skirt, big hoop earrings. I liked this look, until the day he asked me to wear it for him. That was the end of my Paradis phase.

He talked to me about sexual freedom. About the dangers of hard drugs. Sexually transmitted diseases. He bought condoms so I would learn how to put them on. It was the end of the 1980s, the beginning of the 1990s, the AIDS years. There was something in the air, the urge to abolish once and for all the puritanism that had been dynamited in the 1970s, to open the way for all kinds of possible, acceptable, welcome sexualities. In France, libertarian philosophers, artists, and intellectuals signed open letters defending homosexuality and pedophilia and calling for the decriminalization of both, as if those who practiced them were united in their right to unrestricted sexuality for all, as long as all participants, whatever their age, were consenting. They argued for children to be considered as people with free will, able to speak and choose, so they would be liberated from the shackles that have always curbed their desires, made them slaves to adults and their institutions, family, school, hospital, jail. Children should be given back their untamed potential, as if offering them creative power was also about recognizing their right to their sexuality. It is possible that when my stepfather talked to me about and justified our relationship he was inspired by these ideas. But it was not the permissive ideas of the era that forged his words or guided his acts. In a different era he would have said different things. He would always have found a way to justify himself. That's something I discovered, thanks to him, about powerful men, dictators, or even simply people who want more power. They will use any argument they can find. They don't need to invent contexts to suit them, every crisis is good, every absence of crisis is good, everything can be turned in their favor.

Fascination

He was always very charismatic. When he was in prison, he received letters and visits from women he didn't know. While he was in detention pending the trial, he had female admirers, or allies—I don't know what to call them—women who were interested in him and his story, who wanted to help him or save him, I don't know. I suppose it continued after his conviction. There was one woman who visited him often. She had followed the trial and testified in his support. She was the founder and head of a rape survivor's group. During the trial she explained that he was open to dialogue, that he was seeking deep within himself a metamorphosis, that it was rare to see a man like him with such qualities in the dock; basically, that she would have been happy to have an abuser like him.

Serial killers receive a lot of mail. They interest people. Are we fascinated by them? I don't know. I don't think so. We want to understand. They represent something we resist absolutely, the threshold of a place where we cannot or do not want to go.

Thousands of people turned up to the Eichmann

trial. Sorry for bringing this up—I know Eichmann has nothing to do with my story, I'll get back to it. What made so many people want to attend the trial? I think they wanted to see him in person. To interrogate that face. To compare what they knew about what he had done to the truth of the fact that he was, despite everything, just an ordinary human being.

I look at photographs with the same incredulous fascination, wonder how it is possible to see us in family portraits, it must have been real once, it's still real, it's printed on glossy paper, the glaring proof of life, after all that happened, the abuse, the trial, the years in jail, the years of dwelling on it, how time has passed for all of us.

I've got one of these photographs in front of me now, I'd like to reproduce it in the book. I suppose I don't have the right. It would constitute defamation. I'd be prosecuted. Yet all you can see is the six of us looking at the camera. We are all very presentable, more than usually so, we've washed and brushed our hair, we're wearing clean clothes and smiling. There is nothing defamatory about the picture, at least on the face of it.

The photograph says nothing, certainly nothing more than your family snaps, which is why I'd have liked to print it in the book. It could be a slightly staged portrait of any family posing for a snapshot, dad, mom, kids, everyone trying to look at the camera and smile at the same time. There's always one who blinks or looks away. We'll get there in the end. There we go! Thirty years later life has moved on, but they are still there, frozen in time and space, these human beings whose future is a mystery.

What makes this photo interesting is that my mother remembers the day it was taken. It was at a little studio in L'Argentière, my stepfather insisted that we dress up, he had a plan for where everyone should be positioned, he wanted us to look like a happy, well-adjusted family. Don't we look like a lovely little well-adjusted family? Parents in the middle, the two littlest kids in front of them, the two older girls behind. We are all wearing different shades of blue (his color). It must have been spring or summer, we are tanned, our hair is sun-kissed, except for my mother who has just had her hair dyed a not very flattering shade of auburn. She looks pretty, in spite of the awful color. She must be thirty-six or -seven. She is leaning her head on his shoulder and looking straight at the camera. He made a big fuss about her being in that position. It can't have been very comfortable. Her smile looks a little forced. Not surprising, they had just had a fight, she didn't want to smile. She didn't want to have the photograph taken, nor did any of us. He'd yelled at her in the car. No one is at ease, if you look closely at our faces you can see how self-conscious we all are. My youngest sister, who was usually always laughing, looks very serious for a little girl of four or five. She is wearing a pale blue dress and plastic clip-on earrings that she found at the Salvation Army store. She is sitting on her daddy's knee, and her brother, an adorable blond, gap-toothed little boy, looks tense, or maybe he's sleepy, like my teenage sister Rose, standing behind my stepfather in a hooded sweatshirt. They're all smiling, without any great conviction, a bit like people in old photographs who look like they don't know how to pose, snapped in the street, faces vague, thoughts impenetrable. Grave, slightly sad expressions. Except for him and me. He looks untroubled, confident, there's a look of munificence on his relaxed features, he's looking straight ahead in the center of the picture, his arm draped around the littlest one's shoulder. As for me, I look positively carefree. I am fourteen or fifteen. By the time the photograph was taken the rape had stopped. Not long before, I think. It probably happened a few more times, but I knew it was going to stop. Hold the pose, take a picture, one thing more, one thing less, I could care less about anything.

One more smile for the road and that's it, we're done.

I'd asked my mother to send me some family photographs. She scanned this one for me. I told her I was working on an art installation with some girlfriends and a male friend who'd all been raped. She only sent me photos from when I was a teenager, after the abuse had ended. She said she couldn't find any from before.

I was planning to use a bunch of images picked at random. A street party. Skiing. Hiking. On the shore of the Lac de Savines. I couldn't see much difference between them and the staged photo taken by the professional photographer. They're all equally unlikely, equally banal and disturbing. In each case, a few hours before or after the picture was taken, he had led me into a room and I had fellated him. I didn't even have to kneel, it was just him standing and me standing in front of him, because I barely reached his waist.

I keep wondering if I should say *I,* to make it clear that this little girl is also me, now, aged forty-four. Or should

I say *she*, the little girl. I don't know what works better for you. Maybe it's more realistic if I say *she*. Obviously, for me it's me, I don't feel the uncomfortable incongruity some writers talk about when looking at pictures from their past, because I never got out. It's always the present for me. It's always me, it's always now.

I could spend a long time staring at the expression of the man in the photo. I can lose myself in it. What is behind his eyes? What is it that fascinates us about criminals, monsters? We think they hold the clue to one of life's greatest mysteries: evil. We think that because they have done something irreparable, they must at least have learned something. What evil is, or at least, even if they aren't acquainted with the universality of evil through their own misdeeds, presumably they know the specific evil they've chosen. They are on the other side of a border that we will never cross. But we're so often disappointed. There seems to be something banal at the heart of the crime itself, not only because of the nature of those criminals who are driven by impulse, or others who follow orders like sheep. Even genuine monsters, who make the deliberate choice to plunge headlong into darkness, rarely live up to our expectations.

Studies of child abusers show that there is no typical profile beyond the fact that they are, in the vast majority of cases, male. They come from all levels of society, all different countries, all different age ranges. Clinical studies show that there are two principal types of predator: those with dependency and avoidance disorders, characterized by submissiveness, passivity and social isolation, and those who have disorders linked to narcissism, antisocial and psychopathic tendencies that are characterized by power, control, and violence. Those in the former category include people so immature they do not even understand that what they are doing is inappropriate. Those in the latter category are resolving their own profound suffering by dominating a person who is even weaker than they, easier to manipulate than an adult, more likely to become prey. Most perverts belong to that group, but as well as using rape to resolve this internal conflict, they take pleasure from the suffering of their victim. They are manipulators who construct a philosophical system to justify their actions to themselves; they think they are above ordinary morality and law, believe themselves to be superior, and assume responsibility for their acts.

They are the ones who tend to fascinate the public. Perhaps people think they are more interesting, for on the face of it they see things with more clarity, and are more likely to tell us something about the evil they commit and take pleasure in. But in the end they are just as disappointing as those who suffer from some mental disorder or lack, to whom something terrible happened, dogs chasing their own tails. Perverts can talk about themselves for hours, analyzing their own tragedy, even trying to understand the lack of empathy that characterizes them. They find themselves enthralling, and are often simply happy to have an audience. But they rarely have anything new to tell us about what they have done.

Adopting the term *crime*, summoning evil as a horizon, makes it sound very serious. But there are worse things. There are always worse things. It's not like he made me eat my own excrement or forced me to watch him beheading animals. Presumably that explains why the judge handed down a nine-year jail sentence out of a maximum of twenty. It is actually quite a long sentence compared to the usual penalty for child rape, which is more like five years, but in this case it makes sense that he got a longer sentence; there was satisfaction, even pleasure in seeing his victim suffer, and the abuse went on for a long time. But, as I say, it could have been worse. Longer sentences are for the ones who make children eat their own excrement or force them to watch pornographic films showing other children being abused, or prostitute them to friends and neighbors, or keep them chained to the bed, that kind of thing. I can't help wondering, as I read over the last paragraph, if I come across as a bit sarcastic. That is not my intention at all. I do think there is something slightly absurd about trying to make a certain number of years in jail correspond to a crime like this, or maybe even to any crime. What does a period of imprisonment have to do with the theft of a car, or the harm caused to the people whose car has been stolen? What does seven years in an institution funded by the taxpayer achieve—sure, it involves solitude, privation, and shame, but still, what possible correlation could there be with the seven years spent torturing a child? What criterion is used to establish equivalence? In fact, the real question is, are we really seeking equivalence?

On the one hand I agree with the notion of keeping things proportionate and establishing degrees both in terms of suffering and the gravity of the crime. It needn't necessarily correspond to a set number of years in prison, but it seems that it is possible and desirable to acknowledge that some crimes are more serious than others. I'm writing this in 2021, at the very moment when France is debating whether to abolish the statute of limitations for sexual crimes involving children. Those who are against it argue that lifting the statute of limitations should be reserved only for the most extreme cases, crimes against humanity and genocide. I don't know if I agree. Obviously, I know that the rape of an individual, even a child, even though it is abhorrent and even if it went on for years, is not the same as genocide. But is making these crimes subject to the statute of limitations and not others a way of recognizing this difference? The logic of the argument escapes me somewhat.

It's true though, it could have been worse.

I write from a position of privilege, which is not simply that of still being alive. My white privilege (sure, white trash, nothing much to be proud of, but white nonetheless), my nationality and culture. My rape was neither insignificant nor the most horrific, for rape is relative, relative both to the conditions of my birth in the country that invented human rights, and the fact that the crime has been recognized by the guilty party and in the eyes of the law. And the fact I have both the opportunity and the right to write about it today.

I should stop now and let those who need it more than me have their say. These words are aimed toward this silence, a bow pulled taut as the arrow will fly.

But right now, because I am speaking, because I have been offered—or have taken—the opportunity, I am going to keep going until I reach the end.

Portrait of Sammy

My father is in some of the photos too. My beloved papa. Did I make up this love, or embroider it in order to erase the rest? Was this love a life vest I inflated myself, with my puny survivor's breath, prepared to do whatever it took to escape the shipwreck, the tempest that was my childhood? Perhaps.

He visited us every Sunday. He always wore a clean shirt. He tidied up his appearance, his thoughts, combed his wild hair and beard. We'd see him driving up in his old jalopy, the back seats held in place with rope. He'd park in the little parking lot not far from our house. I would keep watch, listening to the passing traffic for the sound of his car, excitedly looking forward to the noise, the regular repetition of his arrival. He always brought lettuce, carrots, radishes from his garden.

He turned up at lunchtime. We ate quietly, virtually in silence, and then we went out for a walk around the neighborhood. There was no need to talk, my sister and I were just happy he was there. We missed him terribly. He missed us too. And during those two hours stolen from the desperation of our other life, despite the crushing presence of our stepfather making conversation, directing operations, passing plates, the meal, determining the route we would take on our walk, everything, despite the monstrous coercive authority he had on us all, we scavenged whatever delicious crumbs we could of the lost paradise of our life with our father, savored them like psychotropic candies that allowed us to superimpose onto the reality of what our lives had become the parallel dimension of the world of happiness that might have been.

Before my mother met my stepfather and we moved into the prison house, we lived a bohemian life with our dropout parents, too young, too free, too unstable, our life rhythmed by an endless series of moves from renovated barns into bedrooms with brown or orange wallpaper at our grandparents and back again. For a year after their separation, after my mother had gone off to find herself, had trained as a mountain guide and taken new lovers, we lived with my father. Later we would be told that the decision for us to go and live with her had been mutual. They had both agreed that our father was unable to take proper care of us, and it would be better for us to have a stable family life with our mother rather than stay with him, living a hand-to-mouth existence. To begin with, they said, things would be a bit of a struggle, we'd have to move out of the rented apartment in the village into the ruined house because we didn't have the money to cover the rent, but the building work wouldn't take long, and we'd soon each have our own comfortable bedroom. There'd be a proper kitchen, and a living room with a woodburning stove to heat the large space.

I don't know exactly when he stopped coming to see us. He was still coming by the time the other children were born, my brother a year after we moved into the house, my sister the year after that. For the first few months we all lived in the basement, then we moved upstairs and for several years all six of us pretty much lived in one large room. My stepfather built an ingenious bunkbed between the kitchen and the living area where my sister and I slept, tucked into the stairwell that one day, supposedly, would lead upstairs to our bedrooms. For a few years my father came to see us every Sunday, and then every other Sunday, and then, gradually, he stopped coming at all.

I picture him with his lettuces, his wool jacket, his heavy boots, pale eyes in a handsome face, lots of hair and a beard. I can still hear his laugh. I hear it in my own laugh, sardonic and sad, that starts like a cascade flowing outward, before it suddenly picks up again, curls inward and ends in a stifled gasp. We laughed all the time when we lived with him. He made bonfires in the front garden, and we toasted cheese and hunks of bread in the evening, even on school nights if we felt like it. We went down to the river and threw branches into the water, then followed them as they floated off on the current. We listened to the radio. We jumped on the bed. He took us to school by sledge in the winter and then, when the snow melted, he took us on his moped. He taught me to read, swim, ride a bicycle. He taught me it was possible to be loved boundlessly without being asked for anything in return. All things that, though I obviously didn't know it at the time, would be of vital use to me later on.

I loved it when he came to visit. But I was always disappointed as well. He represented my escape hatch. I used to tell myself that one day he would take us away with him. He never took us away. Not once, not even for a weekend. He came, spent time with us, left. When I was fourteen, I asked if I could live with him. He said no.

When he found out about the rape, he withdrew into

silence. He didn't come to the trial. He simply let himself die.

People say I look like him. I have his eyes, the same shape face, the way I stand, a certain expression. But I am not like my father. I'm a survivor. I don't know why. I'm not particularly proud of it. I sometimes feel ashamed. I lost the father I adored. I have lost close friends, people who deserve a hundred times more than me to still be alive, to marvel at a sunset. I invent justifications. I tell myself the reason I'm still alive is that I have to tell this, I have to try to lie as little as possible, I mustn't make it less or more ugly than it is. But I know these are just excuses. There is no valid reason I'm here and they are not. And there is nothing about my experience that another person couldn't tell.

I realized that it is not hope that makes us survive. There is no hope, no will: what will could we possibly be talking about. Instinct, some feeling of self-preservation, like a tree, a stone, an animal, wrote Varlam Shalamov in *Kolyma Stories,* after several harrowing years in a gulag. So much for the moral superiority of the survivor.

I'm here. I'm still here. In that sense I'm like him, I'm like my rapist, my educator, my instructor in the perverse and cruel game of life. We have crossed the land of darkness and emerged, not unharmed, certainly, but alive, at least.

I have been living in Mexico for some years. There are stray dogs everywhere here. Female dogs, mostly. People here don't spay their animals, it's costly and they don't need the extra expense. They don't bother to find homes for their litters either, they just abandon the females before they can become attached. They dump them in the wild. You see the bitches on the side of the road, gnawing on carrion, chasing people on bicycles, lazing in the sun. You often see them trying to cross the road. Mostly they get run over and killed. They lie there in the middle of oncoming traffic, no one ever stops to pull them onto the side of the road. But there are a few who make it. There are the crazed ones, threading through the traffic, eyes filled with hostility, heads covered in scabs; then there are the ones who seem indifferent to danger, loping across the road as if they have all the time in the world. You can tell which ones will make it, they're old and mangy with drooping ears, often with some kind of injury, a gimpy leg or a milky eye. They survive. That's all they do. Their main quality is that they are still here despite a prognosis that would give them up for dead. What do they have that the others lack? Nothing, they have nothing more. It's even possible they have some-thing less.

My life as a succession of news items in the local paper

I'd like to be able to say who is the speaking voice here, to distinguish her from me, to make her the speaker of the words, not me. Like a news story, with me as the person to whom it happened. Among the archives of my life that have been preserved, I found a few press cuttings filed away with a handful of old photos. I featured a few times in the press. It's strange to see your name in print, even when it's only the local newspaper. There's that sense of never being entirely only yourself. Everything about you also belongs to the wider social group, which you might strengthen or endanger. You are exposed, in the spotlight, and yet paradoxically you are at the same time erased: The person being written about is not the self you know, but a self that has been doctored and transformed by other people's scrutiny and interpretation.

The article takes up an entire page. It's illustrated by two large photographs, one of a woman born in the same barn back in 1930, the other of my young parents (they were twenty-two and twenty-three) with their newborn baby, looking like Joseph and Mary in the stable. The journalist is rather taken with this analogy, which he turns into a metaphor that runs through the entire piece. The hook for the article is my name. Feigning naivete, he wonders why my parents are not allowed to give me whatever name they like.* He describes the stream he had to cross to reach the abandoned barn where they live; a way of life that is completely at odds with the surrounding society; the unassisted birth of their baby; the life of hardship they have chosen. The mayor of the village has refused to register the baby. It's not clear why. Is it because they have chosen a name that is too strange and unusual, or simply because of who they are?

The journalist talks about lots of other things as well as the baby's name. He describes the back-to-nature existence of the two young dropouts and society's ambivalent feelings toward them. They are perfectly pleasant and innocuous.

---

* Up until 1993 French parents were obliged to name their children from a list of state-sanctioned first names (translator's note).

« NEIGE », c'est l'adorable prénom du premier bébé né au Forest de Vars depuis 47 ans

Le Forest-de-Vars. — En venant de Guillestre, il faut prendre la première route à droite à la sortie de Saint-Marcellin-de-Vars. Deux kilomètres plus loin, on laisse la voiture sur le bas-côté et l'ascension pédestre commence...

... Quinze minutes d'un chemin abrupt, caillouteux et herbeux, à la fois, strié de rigoles alimentées par la fonte des neiges de l'Alpet et de la Mayt, encore tout encapuchonnés de blanc.

Soudain, au détour du chemin, la maison apparaît entre les arbres et dans le grondement du Rebrun dont les eaux bouillonnantes se hâtent vers la vallée.

Un torrent qu'il faut traverser à pieds mouillés, tant pis pour les chaussures de ville, à cette époque de l'année, avant d'arriver dans la cour de la vieille ferme typiquement haut-alpine.

Un grand et beau barbu aux yeux bleus est là, qui fend du bois à la hache. Un peu sur ses gardes, sans doute, mais peut-être un peu timide aussi, sous des dehors volontairement décontractés. Mais bien sympa, tout compte fait, avec ses faux airs de Saint-Joseph.

Pas si faux que ça, après-midi, puisque Sammy Sinno est d'ascendance levantine...

« Entrez donc », lance-t-il en poussant la vieille porte de bois.

Et là, c'est l'émerveillement ! Une petite chose, à la frimousse encore plissée, dans les bras d'une jeune femme dont le visage épanoui porte encore les traces des douleurs de l'enfantement.

« Elle n'a que cinq jours, ma fille », annonce Sylviane Mignot, en s'asseyant sur une vieille chaise branlante, comme si elle devait s'excuser...

Nous sommes au Forest-de-Vars, plus exactement au lieu dit le Rebrun, dans le vieux chalet de montagne, inhabité depuis des lustres, où Sammy et Sylviane sont venus abriter leur amour d'adolescents.

Amour réciproque, mais aussi amour de la nature, de la vraie vie, au contact des choses et des gens du pays — les plus proches sont à quinze minutes de marche — qui les ont, d'emblée, adoptés.

Le plafond bas, de poutres et de ciment mélangés, le sol de grosses planches, le lit de bois et le vieux poêle de fonte dans lequel les flammes dévorent les rondins en ronflant : tout cela ramène cinquante ans en arrière et rappelle les pauvres conditions de vie d'antan.

UNE NAISSANCE « A L'ANCIENNE »

« Nous tenions à ce que notre enfant naisse là où nous nous sommes aimés », disent-ils en baissant les yeux.

Il y est né. Par une belle nuit de printemps, le 22 mai, après quatre heures des inévitables douleurs.

Sylviane et Sammy, qui poussaient leur désir de retour à la nature jusqu'à se méfier des soins modernes, ont refusé toute idée d'une assistance médicale.

Sylviane a mis son enfant au monde sans aide, en la seule présence de Sammy, comme au bon vieux temps. Non sans inquiétude, c'est vite, vécu mais bien lu, depuis qui travaillaient autrefois le ciment avec laquelle Sammy a fiché quatre branches qui lui tiennent lieu de pieds.

POURQUOI PAS NEIGE ?

Dire que les problèmes sont tous résolus serait mentir. Le premier d'entre eux les oppose à l'administration.

« Notre fille, nous l'avons appelée « Neige », puisqu'elle est née au pays de la neige. Et voilà que les bureaucrates du Gap rejettent ce prénom », regrettent nos deux jeunes parents-amoureux.

« Nous connaissons, pourtant, au moins une fille, déjà grande, qui s'appelle Neige sans la moindre histoire.

Serait-on plus rétrograde à Gap qu'ailleurs ? Et puis, Neige est-ce plus maisonnant qu'Euphrasie ou Zoé qui auraient été acceptés sans difficulté ?

Refus encore pour le patronyme. Sammy et Sylviane souhaitaient donner à leur fille leurs deux noms accolés, Sinno-Mignot.

Cette double obstination administrative d'un autre âge surprend et irrite à la fois tous les Varsins qui ont pris fait et cause pour la petite « Boule de Neige ».

QUARANTE SEPT ANS APRES...

Autre aspect, non moins attachant, de cette naissance, là-haut dans la montagne. Au-rait-on appris quelque part à la Forest depuis le 6 mai 1930. Oui, vous avez bien lu, depuis quarante sept ans.

L'avant-dernière née avait été, aussi, une fille. Née, comme Neige sans la moindre assistance médicale. Cela n'a-t-il pas empêché la grandir et de devenir mère de famille : Mme Emilie Benoît, née Rostollan. Elle vit toujours à Vars, à Sainte-Catherine, sur l'autre flanc de la montagne, où nous sommes allés la surprendre dans le chemin creux où, un fichu sur la tête et le traditionnel tricot en mains, elle gardait son troupeau de génisses.

« Ils ont bien du courage, ces jeunes », nous a-t-elle dit sur le ton de l'admiration. Autant que les anciens « Forestiers » qui, pourtant ont tous déserté le Forest les uns après les autres »...

LUCIEN DAUTRIAT

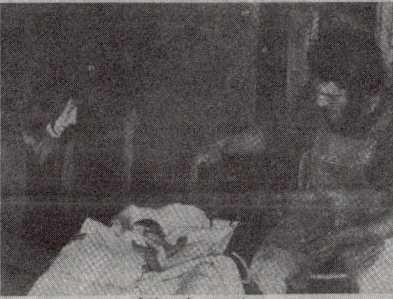

Nos photos. — Neige », une mignonne petite fille entre son papa et sa maman nous le regard d'une mère poule qui n'avait jamais vu de bébé.

Emilie Rostollan, maintenant Mme Benoît, est née, quarante sept avant, au Forest.

Le Dauphiné libéré, 3rd June 1977.

Yet their obstinate rejection of the kind of lives that other people seek to build appears to be threatening. Is this the reason everyone is standing in their way?

A few days later the newspaper returns to the subject of the baby's first name, with a letter from a reader pointing out that the Duke of Parma's daughter is also called Neige and no one has any problem with that. The name triggers issues of class and power; it is an ideological, almost existential battle that will leave wounds on both sides.

I thought of the ghosts that lodge within names, Maylis de Kerangal writes with a note of melancholy. Names and words bear traces that are not the same for everyone. By naming our ghosts, might we perhaps manage to free ourselves of them, a little?

Our parents wanted to give us names that had nothing to do with any genealogy. Neige and Rose: names that evoke the life force of nature rather than any lineage or culture or religion, names that would belong only to us, something that begins rather than perpetuates, something like the new world to which they aspire. In a way, this is a story about names. My mother never married my father. She tried to give us her family name, she thought it only fair that her name should continue to exist through us, she didn't see why she should have to give it up for a man or for social convention. Once again, the authorities refused to allow her what they were happy to allow other people.

The fight over names ended with my stepfather. My mother capitulated, I don't know why, presumably another consequence of the hold he had over her. They got married and she took his name. The two children they had together bore his surname, and their first names were chosen by him as well. My brother came within a hair's breadth of being called Johnny.

A year or so after the trial she divorced my stepfather and went back to using her maiden name. Whenever she mentions him now, she always identifies him by his surname, presumably to distance herself from him. I am unable to utter that name without feeling as though I am summoning an evil spirit. Rose says she feels her whole body stiffen when she hears the sounds that make up the name, as if they harbor the threat of his presence.

He tried to exercise control over us through language. He wanted us to call him papa. And he wanted to give us nicknames too, the way some families use private names to reinforce the closeness and intimacy of the group. I suppose that was the argument he used, nicknames are an expression of love, a way of showing we're tighter with each other than with the outside world. Except it was very clear that this thing about nicknames was another way of exerting power over us; the ridiculous pet names he chose left us in no doubt about that. He wanted to call me Néné and my sister Roro. It must have been a power game to humiliate our father for the names he'd chosen when we were born. To change Neige and Rose to Néné and Roro. But we stood our ground. I don't really know how. It must have been a long and bitter struggle, but eventually he gave up. We never called him papa, and we kept our names. We won the battle. But we lost on other fronts. On all the other fronts.

There is a photo of me in my second appearance in the newspaper too, wearing a headlamp and perched at the front of what looks like an inflatable dinghy or small row-boat. I'm nearly sixteen. One of my mother's childhood friends, an amateur caver, had organized a trip with the local youth center. As the journalist notes in his write-up of an underground adventure that was more Famous Five than Jules Verne, we were more frightened than ever in actual danger:

PLUS DE PEUR QUE DE MAL !

En cette matinée du 6 mars, le Spéléo-Club de la MJC de Belle-garde organisait une excursion à la grotte des Huguenots. C'était la cinquième visite proposée aux curieux du monde souterrain dans le cadre de la quinzaine spéléo. Le petit groupe composé de huit personnes était guidé par le dynamique et sympathique jeune président, Ivan Ragon. Il y avait là des hommes d'âge mûr (comme quoi, il n'est jamais trop tard pour taquiner l'aventure...) et deux jeunes et charmantes demoiselles : Neige et Florence. Après une petite et agréable marche d'approche dans la nature ensoleillée, le groupe parvient à l'entrée. Chacun s'équipe, Ivan donne les instructions pour la manipulation des lampes à acétylène et en avant ! La première partie s'effectue sans problèmes. Pour certains, c'est un baptême et le franchissement du seuil ne s'est pas fait sans appréhension. Cette grotte, bien que réputée pour l'initiation est de difficulté moyenne. Il y a un petit lac à franchir en deux fois et quelques passages d'escalade. Ce qui peut paraître élémentaire en plein jour l'est beaucoup moins dans le noir et l'humidité. Arrivé au lac, Ivan gonfle un petit dingy. Les deux demoiselles embarquent d'abord et Ivan, qui est équipé pour entrer dans l'eau jusqu'aux épaules les pousse doucement jusqu'à l'autre rive à une vingtaine de mètres, puis revient chercher les autres explorateurs. Ceux-ci pas-

Cette petite croisière souterraine leur a fait découvrir de magnifiques concrétions et un vestige de pont de calcite. La seconde partie du franchissement du lac sera plus courte, mais plus cocasse. Il n'y avait cette fois qu'une dizaine de mètres de traversée. La même opération fut répétée, mais, au moment d'accoster en face les deux filles se penchèrent du même côté et firent chavirer leur esquif. Il n'y avait aucun danger, sauf celui de mouiller sa montre. Les deux spéléos en herbe en furent quittes pour un petit bain d'eau fraîche et un moment d'émotion. Cette péripétie déclencha l'hilarité générale, y compris celle des représentants du sexe "dit faible". Pour un baptême, c'en était un ! Qui osera encore dire que les jeunes ne se mouillent pas !... Le groupe poursuivit son exploration comme prévu jusqu'au siphon terminal. Au delà du siphon, ce n'est plus une affaire de novices et pourtant c'est là que commence la partie la plus vaste de la grotte (mais pas la plus jolie). Le voyage de retour se déroula sans incident cette fois. Cependant, les deux baigneuses se hâtèrent de retrouver les voitures pour mettre des vêtements secs. Le soleil était chaud, l'air était doux, ce fut une bonne matinée dont tous garderont un bon souvenir.

La Tribune républicaine du Pays de Gex, 11th March 1993.

During the underground cruise they were able to admire magnificent stalactites and stalagmites, and the remains of a calcite bridge. The second part of the lake crossing was shorter, but rather more comical. It was no more than a dozen meters to get across, but just as they reached the other side the two girls leaned over the same side of the boat and tumbled into the water. The two young spelunkers were never in any danger, apart from getting their watches wet; they got away with a very chilly dip and a bit of a shock. The incident set off general hilarity, including among the representatives of the so-called "weaker sex."

In 1993 the internet didn't exist yet. People read the regional press to find out what was going on in the world, the region, the village, the date of the pottery market, the racing results. And, of course, human interest stories. It was neat to be featured there, in pages filled with small or major local disasters, moments of shared joy and fun. I only vaguely remember falling into the lake, but I have a strong memory of that descent deep under the ground, the silence of the cave, its dank, clammy walls that seemed almost alive, like a strange, narrow tunnel leading to the secret center of the world.

Why am I writing about this here? Do you think it has nothing to do with anything? You're right, it has nothing to do with anything, it's just proof from the last century, presented in a flowery and charming style, that victims of sexual abuse are also ordinary people who like climbing, swimming, caving. Maybe they once fell in an underground lake and got their socks wet.

7 ans de calvaire pour une fillette

HAUTES-ALPES. Le nouveau mari de sa mère en avait fait son "objet sexuel" alors qu'elle n'avait que 9 ans ! Durant près de sept années, la fillette a dû subir sans relâche agressions sexuelles et viols. Aujourd'hui majeure, elle s'est confiée et sa mère a déposé plainte. Le "beau père" a été écroué hier

Chaque fois que l'on prend connaissance de tels faits, les mots manquent pour exprimer la colère, l'émotion et l'indignation ressenties. Ils manquent aussi sûrement pour qualifier leur auteur, un homme de 39 ans, écroué, hier matin, à la maison d'arrêt de Gap. Durant six années dans un village de la Vallouise, cet individu a agressé et violé la fillette de sa femme (1), de façon régulière et sordide. L'enfant avait 9 ans à peine lorsque le nouveau compagnon de sa mère a commencé ses agissements. Dès 12 ans, il lui imposait des relations sexuelles, lesquelles n'auront cessé que lorsque la jeune fille aura atteint un certain degré de maturité. Son calvaire remonte en fait à la fin des années 80 et au début de cette décennie.

Aujourd'hui majeure, poursuivant des études dans une grande métropole régionale, la jeune femme n'a plus été en mesure de garder son terrible secret, de porter seule ce lourd fardeau. Il y a quelques mois, elle s'est confiée à sa mère, ouvrant par là même (en révélant les agissements de son "beau père") une plaie immense au niveau de la structure familiale.

Il aura fallu alors plusieurs mois à cette mère pour assumer le choc. De son second mariage et au fil des ans sont nés en effet deux enfants... Finalement, au début de ce mois, et après mûre réflexion, la mère s'est rendue au parquet de Gap. Et à parlé, déposant plainte entre les mains de la justice. Immédiatement, le substitut du procureur de la République, Michel Rodon, a saisi les gendarmes de la brigade de recherche de Briançon. En deux semaines, faisant preuve de diligence, de perspicacité mais aussi de beaucoup de tact, les enquêteurs ont multiplié les investigations et les auditions.

Finalement, ces dernières heures ils ont interpellé le "beau père"... lequel a entièrement reconnu les faits. Pour seuls arguments de défense, l'homme a invoqué les "difficultés relationnelles" éprouvées avec la fillette lorsqu'il s'est mis en ménage puis marié avec sa mère. Il considérait que c'était là "le seul moyen pour lui de rentrer en relation" avec l'enfant.

Guide en saison d'été, il jouissait semble-t-il d'une excellente réputation dans la vallée et plus particulièrement au village où la famille réside. Hier matin, après que le parquet de Gap eut ouvert une information judiciaire, l'individu a été présenté au juge d'instruction, en l'occurrence à Mᵐᵉ Louis, assurant l'intérim. Celle-ci lui a signifié sa mise en examen du chef de "viols sur mineurs" de moins de 15 ans "par personne ayant autorité".

Un crime et des circonstances aggravantes qui sont passibles de la cour d'assises et pour lesquels ce beau-père indigne encourt jusqu'à 20 ans de réclusion criminelle.

Jean BEVERAGGI

(1) Rappelons une nouvelle fois que le fait de ne pas révéler dans nos colonnes l'identité de la personne mise en examen (et bénéficiant jusqu'à son jugement de la présomption d'innocence) dans cette sordide affaire, relève de la seule nécessité, dictée par la loi et le bon sens, de protéger la victime et ses proches.

Le Dauphiné libéré, June 2000

In my third appearance in the paper, there is no photograph. No names either. But everything is there nonetheless.

It is hard to simply relate the facts. Beyond his indignation, evident from the exclamation mark in the subtitle and the way he puts the word *stepfather*, referring to a man so contemptible he doesn't know what to call him, in quotation marks, the journalist can't help but express certain preconceptions of the time. According to him, the girl has spoken out in order to free herself of her *terrible secret*. One might imagine that the girl is in a much better place now she has said it, now that she has shared her *heavy burden* with others. It is not written anywhere in the proceedings of the trial that I spoke out to free myself, quite the opposite: From the beginning I firmly maintained that I was speaking out to protect the others, but still everyone carried on thinking I had done it for myself, and by extension, that I had even sacrificed my family to some extent for my own ends.

I am the person to whom this happened. Who is the *I* speaking here? The woman who the baby daughter of the hippie dropouts in the Alps grew up to become? The caver of the weaker sex who fell into the lake? The little girl whose ordeal lasted seven years, who finally freed herself of her terrible burden by writing a poignant memoir? You could argue that it doesn't matter who's speaking, whose mind this narrative has sprung from. But it wouldn't be the same, depending on which life it sprang from. I am all three of those girls, and more. I carry all their voices within me.

My life as a horror film

I have pure and simple nightmares where he is coming after me to rape me. I try to hide or distract him with meaningless chatter. Sometimes he catches me and rapes me. Sometimes it's just me, running, fleeing, cries stuck in my throat.

I have this dream where my little sister, in her child's body but with her adult way of speaking, is telling me he didn't rape her, but he touched my brother's playmates when they came for a sleepover. I am desperately trying to find all these children, running panting through the narrow back streets of a village I don't recognize. I wake up with my heart thumping.

There are the semi-erotic dreams where something sexual is going on in an unlikely place, a meeting or a date in a place it ought to be shocking to be naked, though we don't seem at all bothered, I approach my partner, he has his back to me or he's in profile or in shadow, I thought it was my lover, I see his face, a grinning mask, it's him.

Mostly the dreams are more David Lynch than horror, a palpable sense of dread, unremitting and oppressive, pervading each scene as it unfolds. I know from the start that he is there. He will always be there. Watching, waiting for the moment to come into view.

My life as an American melodrama

I'm from a modest background. My parents are rural hippies, then after my mother marries my stepfather we become downright poor. My mother, stepfather, and we four children—I'm the oldest of three girls and a boy—inhabit a half ruin that's in a constant process of being fixed up. My mother cleans houses, my stepfather is a laborer on construction sites. After the first few years of abuse my body starts to give in, I am diagnosed with acute scoliosis. I spend long periods of time in a specialist clinic. My skinny frame is wrapped in a little corset like Frida Kahlo's that functions as a support to help me grow straight despite my spine having got off to a bad start, no one suspects why, it's grown all twisted as if under the weight of a monstrous burden. But I don't let it defeat me. I work hard at school. The teachers notice and encourage me to keep it up. I do well in my exams. I leave home for university. I go first to Nice, then to Marseille, and later, on an exchange program, to the United States. With the help of my new student friends, who are better educated and supported, I come to understand that I must denounce my rapist, in order to protect the other children and demand justice. I tell my mother, who takes a long time to reflect before she eventually agrees to join me in filing a complaint with the police. There's a trial, he's found guilty and sent to prison where he belongs. The little ones are safe for a few years. I am free. I go back to America then move to Mexico. I complete a doctorate in literature. I write some books. I meet a nice man. We have a child. One day I tell my daughter what happened to me when I was a little girl. She finds it inconceivable, it's light years from her own experience. Another day, years from now, she's an adult and I'm practically an old woman, she reads this book in which I describe this horrific period of my life. We are sitting on a terrace looking out over the magnificent landscape. We watch as the mist creeps over a distant hill opposite our house in Michoacán in Mexico, the childhood home she left when she went to study abroad. She comes back from time to time to see her elderly parents. She takes my hand in hers. She cries a bit, but I don't cry. I am happy.

A happy ending

What I've just recounted is the version with the happy ending. But obviously there isn't really a happy ending. There can never be a happy ending for someone who was abused as a child. It is a mistake and a source of suffering to believe in the myth of the survivor like you see in the movies. It makes you believe in linear time, that there's a straightforward progression from victim to accuser to survivor to a person who is happy. But the reality—we can go all the way back to pre-Columbian times, to the ancient Greeks, at least as far back as Heraclitus to demonstrate this—is that we have always understood time as cyclical, going round and coming back for all eternity. There is no finale, it is simply a question of the script—the movie has to end at some point. Don't be surprised then, if you're a survivor, you've done a lot of work on yourself, you're doing pretty well actually, as well as can be expected given how things started out for you, maybe you're doing remarkably well, and yet you're not happy. You don't have that sense of peace that the actress portraying me feels, sitting in a chair next to my daughter, whose life hasn't been entirely without pain and suffering but at least there was no sexual abuse in her childhood. And there's a good reason you don't have it. I don't have the slightest inkling of a happy ending either. Because it isn't over. Not for me, not for you, not for anyone. And as long as there is any child on earth still suffering abuse, it will never be over for any of us.

Still, it's true that once you can talk about the trauma, it means you have been slightly set free. But this does not mean that words or literature function as therapy. Quite the opposite: Writing can only happen once the work, or part of the work, has been done, that part of the work that consists of emerging from the tunnel. *You don't write with your neuroses*, as Gilles Deleuze puts it. *Neurosis and psychosis are not stages of life, but states into which we fall when the process is interrupted, prevented, or blocked. Illness is not a process, but a halt to the process.*

That famous line of Antonin Artaud that people always seem to quote at the drop of a hat, the one where he says that no one ever wrote, painted, sculpted, modeled, built, or invented except to escape hell, is perhaps a dreadful misconception. The reality is the opposite: The person who writes, draws, and so on has already emerged from hell, which is precisely why they can write. Because when you're in hell you can't talk about anything, you can't invent things, you're too busy just being in hell.

If it is possible to talk about it, writes Virginia Woolf, it is because the event is detached from the actual suffering, which is experienced on the level of unreality. It only becomes real once it has been captured in language:

> *I hazard the explanation that a shock is at once in my case followed by the desire to explain it. I feel that I have had a blow; but it is not, as I thought as a child, simply a blow from an enemy hidden behind the cotton wool of daily life; it is or will become a revelation of some order; it is a token of some real thing behind appearances; and I make it real by putting it into words. It is only by putting it into words that I make it whole; this wholeness means that it has lost its power to hurt me; it gives me, perhaps because by doing so I take away the pain, a great delight to put the severed parts together. Perhaps this is the strongest pleasure known to me.*

Tell the truth, the whole truth, nothing but the truth

During the fourteen-hour trial, before the horrified eyes of my friends, my family, neighbors from the village, some of my old teachers, and even a few complete strangers who have heard that the trial of a man who raped a little girl is being held that day at the Assize Court in Gap and for some reason they've decided to attend, he confesses to a large number of the allegations. He has already been cross-examined, but everything must be repeated in the courtroom. Precise details are required. The frequency of the abuse, the gradual escalation of the sex acts, the things he said while he was raping me, what he did to ensure no one suspected what was going on, what he was thinking, how he imagined putting an end to the whole thing except that he never put it into practice because it kept starting up again. He put a lot of detail into his confession that day, in front of everyone, as if the confession were taking place at a site of repentance. He says that sometimes it was every day, other times a whole month would go by with nothing. He says there was love, that he made sure I got pleasure out of it. And in all this outpouring there's one insane night I remember distinctly which he refuses to corroborate. Am I making it up? But why would I make up that one thing and not the rest? I remember one night but maybe it went on for several nights. My mother wasn't home. I think it was the year my grandfather died. She went away for a few days, maybe a week, to be at his bedside with her sisters. If that is when it happened, it's easy to date, I was twelve. He died of throat cancer a few months later. He breathed his last in a white bed, adrift in the middle of a room cluttered with furniture and memories that he no longer recognized. The rest of us were back at home. My stepfather made me sleep in his bed at night. In my memory it snowed a lot, there was an unusual amount of snow. He said that if there was an avalanche in the mountains above the village, we'd be safe in the bedroom on the ground floor, we'd be safe even if the rest of the house was swept away. It was bizarre, the idea that I was warm and safe in the house but at the same time a prisoner, trapped in the place of safety that was meant to protect me from the cold, from danger, from death. I was at his disposal.

It is an endless orgy of violation. I'll spare you the details, apart from one particularly sordid one, I'm sorry. He gets me down on my hands and knees and tries to sodomize me. He can't get it in. He goes to fetch something, gives me a moment of respite in the dark, comes back in. He spreads Vaseline on my anus and pushes something hard into it. It's so as not to hurt me, he explains, because it won't go in. He goes on for ages, pushing into me, I see them the next day in the garbage, carrots and zucchini that he pushed into my anus to make room for his penis which, he acknowledges with a certain pride, is not a bad size. When it's over I go to the bathroom, there's blood on the toilet paper, I'm almost pleased to see the blood, because now he can't pretend nothing happened, I'm bleeding, it's bad.

He has confessed to many of the things I said happened. Sometimes I wasn't sure I was remembering right, but he confirmed I was. This time it's so clear in my head, I can describe it with absolute certainty, but he denies it. In front of all these people, I stand up and again I describe what he did with the zucchini, the Vaseline and the carrots, because I know it happened, and I know that if I am to heal I have to know what did and didn't happen. Up until this point he has been quite helpful in the process of piecing it all together, given that he could have denied everything and then no one would have believed me. So why deny the sodomy and not the rest? Is it because it's worse? Or he thinks it is? I imagine at this point you're beginning to grasp what I'm getting at. He does think it's worse, he thinks it is infinitely worse than all the other acts, because it happened to him.

It is possible that I'm wrong, again. Perhaps the reason he ends up telling how he was raped when he was a teenager during one of his confessional cross-examinations is simply because he hopes it might mean he will be sentenced more leniently. In studies on the impact of traumatic past events on repeat offenders, researchers have to take this factor into account: Because people believe so strongly in the impact of the cycle of violence on a perpetrator and consider the fact of having been a victim as a mitigating factor, many defendants will make reference to something that happened to them during their own childhood.

My stepfather says the memory came back to him during his pretrial detention, after a session with a police detective or psychologist during which he'd talked about his adolescence. He says it was the priests from the church where he spent extended periods of time, at summer camp and catechism. Maybe it was a male teacher from his Catholic junior high school. There was an investigation into accusations against the priests by other victims, which made his version of events plausible, but either because too much time had elapsed or because he had decided not to press charges the case had not been pursued. Is he thinking now that if he too was a victim he will be treated differently, not merely as a straightforward criminal? I can't be sure of his motivation. He took a while to bring up the episode, as if he needed a period of reflection. It's not as if he portrayed himself from the start as a victim who raped because he was raped. And he doesn't really dwell on it, as if he prefers the shame of being a rapist to the shame of having been raped.

His description of the abuse is hazy, a young priest, a dark room, school desks. He remembers the pain, both physical and spiritual, his absolute silence, he even remembers doubting the truth of the memory, burying it. I've read his words in the transcript of the trial. It seems credible, not only the facts themselves but the way he recounts them, in the classic style of trauma.

I've read several studies that indicate around twenty percent of child rapists were themselves victims of sexual abuse as children. A figure only slightly higher than the incidence of abuse in the overall population. The studies suggest that although there is a strong belief in the victim-perpetrator cycle among the general population, the fact of having been a victim as a child, while clearly a risk factor, is neither a necessary nor a sufficient condition for becoming in turn a perpetrator.

If you had been on the jury, what would you have made of this? Does it make him more or less guilty of rape if he was sodomized by a priest ten or twelve times over a period of a few months? Does this tilt the number of years in jail upward or downward?

Here it is again, that little tone of bravado that emerges every so often. As if all this, the very fact that I'm writing this book, is the reader's fault. As if the reader is another juror, different, but not dissimilar to the ones I've already had to deal with.

It's not as if the members of the jury had requested to be there either. You're expected to do jury service to fulfill your responsibility as a citizen, you accept out of a sense of civic duty, like being asked to count the votes after an election or attend a special meeting of the city council, and there you are in the town of Gap, in a Formule 1 budget hotel with a bunch of other people who also have no idea what the day holds, and then, after a measly breakfast and an information session about how the justice system works, you're taken to the Assize Court where over the course of several hours all the details of my case will be unleashed on you, and you are going to have to decide, collectively, what should be done next.

The accused's attorney is allowed to dismiss two or three members of the jury without knowing anything about them. The attorney bets on the fact that in general women and young people are more likely to empathize with the victim. These people are allowed to leave. They are released from this trial. I don't know if they go home afterward, but I doubt it. Now that they are fulfilling their civic duty, they've made the journey and taken the train and stayed in a Formule 1 budget hotel, I imagine they will be sent to serve on the jury for another trial. As for the ones who stay, who are more likely to be men and to be older, they will have to listen to the double account of these rapes, they'll be spared no detail, from the point of view of both parties, accuser and accused. They can't shut the book, wishing there were fewer descriptions of sex scenes or that the accused was given less time to speak. They are going to have to listen right to the end and come to an informed opinion, because what happens next depends on their interpretation.

I know you're not a juror. If you are holding this book in your hands, there's a decent chance that you're on my side, maybe you are so on my side that you might as well have written this book yourself. It's a safe space, a space with no enemies. I don't need to convince anyone of anything. So what's the point, if we've been in agreement about everything since the beginning?

Reasons for not wanting to write this book

1) I don't want to specialize in rape literature.
2) I'm generally wary of books that deal with topics, which would be a bit difficult to avoid here. How to write something new, something with aesthetic value, if you are crushed by the topic itself?
3) I'd like to do something else, to think about something else, to have a life that is centered on something else.
4) Many books are published every year by survivors. Mostly fiction. Whenever I come across one, I always like to flip through it. Some are very well written, some not. Either way I read them with the same eye. I am looking for a precise

description of the facts. I want to know exactly what he did, how many times, where, what he said, and so on. I loathe the idea that someone might open this book and try to find exactly what was done to me, where he put his cock, and then close it again having found out nothing more than this bizarre fact.

5) I am not sure I have anything at all to offer victims and their families, or perpetrators, or even just someone who wants a better understanding of the subject.

6) I am not sure that the book offers me anything, either as a human being or as a writer.

7) I don't believe in writing as therapy. And even if I did, the idea of healing myself with this book appalls me.

If it is neither for other people nor for me, what is the point?

On top of all this, I agree with the social scientist Dorothée Dussy, who studies incest from an anthropological perspective and argues that the best way to consider these narratives is not head-on but obliquely. If the person talking was affected but they were not the primary victim, their account offers a way of discussing incest as a social phenomenon while avoiding the unbearable pathos of direct suffering. This is how she explains the widespread interest in two recent works that have had significant repercussions in France by offering a way out of the paralysis and denial that afflicts wider society when it comes to discussing this issue, *The Familia Grande*, a memoir by Camille Kouchner, and *Or Maybe One Night*, a podcast presented by the journalist Charlotte Pudlowski:

They have made it possible to talk about incest, the mecha-
nism of silence, the fact that it is a driver and an organizing
mechanism of the whole family, not only the victim and
the perpetrator of the incest. In first-person narratives it is
impossible to see things other than from the narrator's per-
spective, it is always about two people with whom only a
victim or perpetrator of incest can identify. But it is possible
to identify with the sister or brother or child of a victim.

The success of Kouchner's book (aside from the fact that the story she tells is about famous people) is certainly due to this perspective. It takes the reader away from the eye of storm—where it is too dark and blinding, making it impossible to see beyond it—to consider incest as a societal phenomenon. Charlotte Pudlowski's excellent podcast establishes a similar distance; she is affected by and close to her subject—it is her mother who was the victim—but also able to maintain the distance of an indirect witness. She analyzes the phenomenon of incest as a shock wave that has an impact on every member of the family, over generations, and thus also affects wider society. I agree that this is the appropriate distance. That cursed pair, that claustrophobic, fucked-up victim-perpetrator duo, has surely had its day.

I remember how I felt watching Tim Roth's 1999 movie *The War Zone*, in which it is the victim's brother who discovers the rape. The boy is constantly questioning his status as witness, and the audience sees everything through his eyes. He observes, films, interprets signs, watches scenes through cracks in the walls. He is both voyeur and clair-voyant, who ends up able to translate the images into words. He is the mediator who succeeds in breaking the silence. He is in just the right place, neither too close nor too distant.

In "Un trago de aceite," an extraordinary short story by the Mexican writer Antonio Ortuño, a boy narrates a tragicomic tale in which his father, a fruit seller, a charlatan, a bit of a rogue, takes the child to spend the weekend with a bourgeois family in their house in the countryside. The boy is ill at ease with the other children who all look down on him, apart from a girl his own age who is friendlier than the others and seems impressed when he tells her he won a writing prize at school. As he is looking for a place to hide so as not to have to go out on a boat on the lake with the drunken parents, their sneering children, and his own father who embarrasses him with his crude attempts at pretending he's one of them, he stumbles upon one of the fathers molesting the girl. The furious man forces the boy to undress and lashes the two children with his belt. None of the other adults is aware of anything amiss. They come back tipsy from the boat trip and the weekend continues. As they are saying goodbye, the girl addresses the boy:

> —*You write, she said slowly, awkwardly, as if she could barely move her tongue.*
> *I didn't know what to say.*
> —*Write about it one day. In a book . . . Let them read it. Let them tear out the pages. Let them eat them.*

They make a silent promise, and never see each other again. We don't know if the narrator became a writer, if he wrote this story, but we assume he must have done, because we are reading it. He committed to writing because he promised, and because he witnessed. He does not have the right to forget. To say nothing would be a betrayal. I wish I could write this book with a little more distance, to be simply the person who witnessed something, who was touched by the concentric circles of the repercussions, someone whom someone else made promise to write a book to avenge them.

I wish I could distance myself like that, for obvious reasons, but that is not the hand I was dealt.

The one who bears the trace

Once, when I was little, my stepfather told me that it was thanks to him I did so well in school. It was because of what he did to me that I was special. My intelligence, my precocious intellectual ability, came from experiencing something extraordinary that pushed me beyond my limits.

Christine Angot recounts how her abusive father suggested that she write about the incest he had subjected her to. *You should write about what you experienced with me . . . It's interesting. It's not something that everybody experiences.*

He even had an opinion about how she should go about writing it: *The reader should question themselves, wonder whether it is dream or reality, it should be a little hazy, a bit like Robbe-Grillet.*

That's another reason why it's hard to write about this. Not because it brings back painful memories (a person who was abused as a child has no need for a book to bring back painful memories, they are lying in wait every morning upon waking), but because the text, into which the author pours so much effort and will, years of reading, her heart and soul, is, from the very start, the abuser's project, he is right at the heart of it, he almost predicted it, even almost hoped for it.

A person rapes in order to exist. Perhaps they don't know that until it happens (I happen to think they do know, most of the time) but once it has happened it's obvious that this irreparable act will mark for life the victim, the world. It is an act that engenders power, a power that extends far beyond the perpetrator.

Several years ago I learned about a recently uncovered child pornography ring called *damagedforlife*. This was not the name of a victim therapy group, but a site on the dark web passed among predators who are aroused by the knowledge that the acts they are watching involve genuine victims whose lives will be damaged forever. The victim as a person does not exist for them, these people are entirely devoid of empathy, or at least they have a bizarre kind of empathy that doesn't allow them to imagine the victim's suffering experienced from the other side. The victim exists for them simply as a vehicle that will permanently bear the trace of their abuse.

Damaged for life. This book is the proof. I want it to exist, but I hope it doesn't have too many readers. It would mean existing in literature not for my writing but for my subject. The thing I have always dreaded. And that it should be of all things *this* subject, which I did not choose, or want, or create. It would mean existing in literature not because of something I have done but because of something that someone did to me. A nightmare.

And yet I am going to write it anyway, in a kind of senseless rebellion. Take the bull by the horns and drive it completely mad. Fill it with words until it cracks, begs me to stop, and leaves me in peace, at last.

A true story of monstrous deception

Emmanuel Carrère's book *The Adversary* came out in 2000, a year before the trial, when my stepfather was being held in pretrial custody, innocent until proven guilty. It is a work of creative nonfiction about a man called Jean-Claude Romand, who murdered his wife, parents and two children when the lie around which his entire life revolved was about to be revealed. As a young medical student, Romand had failed to turn up for one of his exams. He told everyone he'd passed, and from that moment on, it's never entirely clear why, although the book's main focus is on this strange fork in the road of one man's destiny, it was one lie after another: First he led people to believe he had got his degree, then that he had found a job, and eventually he was commuting daily to Geneva to his office at the WHO. Friends and relatives entrusted him with their savings which he said he deposited for them in private Swiss banks, and that is how he lived for eighteen years, until the crime.

I read the book after my mother recommended it, or maybe after I heard her talking about it. For her, the book was about a monstrous, chilling character whose story she thought was not unlike that of my stepfather. I remember being dismayed by this interpretation, which only intensified the anger I felt toward her. Yes, Carrère's book is about a man who commits a crime, but it's really about a man who lies to everyone he knows for such a very long time. The question at the heart of the book that everyone asks is how could he have lied like that without anyone ever suspecting? How did no one realize? How can a lie lodge itself in the heart of someone's life and become a kind of truth because it does not prevent that life from continuing? Clearly my mother read into the book the questions she was asking herself. For as far as she was concerned, the central betrayal of which my stepfather was guilty was the lie. How had he deceived her for so long without her suspecting anything? I think the story of the Romand family reassured her—all those other people had also let themselves be hoodwinked. Like her, they had never guessed a thing.

What offended me then, and still does, is precisely this: She saw my stepfather first and foremost as a liar. What's so fascinating about Romand is not his horrific crime, the fact that he shot his children in the face, but his ability to make people believe his lies. My mother identified with the innocent people around him who were deceived and betrayed by the fake doctor. Her partner had raped her young daughter over a period of several years, and yet she thought of him not as a rapist but as a liar.

She saw her story everywhere, just as I did mine. At the time I saw this egotism as both natural (everything depends on where you stand) and cruel (but nature is cruel, after all). I know it wasn't indifference to my suffering or to the crime itself, but rather what is known clinically as denial. Even in the midst of the process of coming to terms with the facts there are multiple strategies of denial, and my mother's way of seeing things is one of them. She would rather focus on the lie, which is horrible of course, but less horrible than the thing behind the lie, the thing that the lie conceals. What was so strange about Jean-Claude Romand's lie was that it concealed nothing, it concealed a void. What my stepfather was concealing, to which my mother does not allude—because what she is thinking when she says the word *lie* is the lie he told her about being trustworthy, a good father, occasionally unfaithful maybe, but he loved her—was what he was doing to me at night.

Cruelty and denial are not incompatible. It is not as if on the one hand there's a refusal to see, and on the other the impossibility of seeing. A conscious refusal and an unconscious refusal. An innocent refusal and a guilty refusal. It is possible that there is a little bit of both in a mother's blindness, or a strange interplay between the two: She knows but she doesn't know, she doesn't know but she does know.

I am hard on my mother. I think I have the right to be. She deserves it. But she was not wrong: Truth and lies are indeed the crux of the problem. I am writing this book as a way of trying to get at the truth. A truth that is difficult to determine, difficult to formulate, that goes beyond appearances. The truth doesn't entirely cancel out the other side, the good side, the moments of happiness, the family photographs, but it alters the nature of it, it is its dark side, its cursed twin.

I am hard on my mother. I imagine the reader will be hard on her too. It's a cultural reflex when it comes to stories about incest. We often blame the mother who failed to protect her child more than the rapist himself. It's true, she didn't protect me. Nor did my father. Nor did my grandparents, my uncles and aunts, friends of the family. Nor did my teachers, or the people who worked at the youth center, or the personnel at the hospitals where I spent time being treated for my back, or the psychologists, therapists, and practitioners of alternative medicine I was sent to see. No one protected me. Yes, the mother is guilty. I agree. I have not spared her during the many cycles of anger and recrimination that have taken place over the years. But she wasn't the one who raped me.

When she found out, when I told her one day as we sat in the car, she was dumbstruck, she couldn't think, she couldn't grasp what I was saying. She couldn't believe it. The first thing she did after she parked the car was go inside and ask my stepfather if it was true. She stayed with him for another year. She said she had no choice, she had to finish her nursing studies so she could afford to take care of my brother and sisters. I blamed her, but she wasn't the one who raped me. She filed a complaint to the police, she divorced him, she lost her house and her reputation in the village and in the eyes of her friends. Her life fell apart. Everything she'd done up until then lost all meaning. She didn't stop being a hippie, she still thinks we mustn't dwell too much on bad things, or curse out loud, we should be able to express clearly what we want, petition the universe for help with the things we can't cope with. And yet, in spite of her mystical inclinations, the wise counsel she plucked from the Four Agreements of Toltec wisdom, she did send me the photographs and documents I asked for, the ones she couldn't bear to look at. I'm sure she'll read this book with empathy and kindness and will always stand by me.

"Her life fell apart."

It's easy enough to write. A few words, then on to the next thing. But try and imagine what it actually means. To live for fourteen years with someone you're deeply in love with, someone you love so much you're ready to have two more children with him, though you already have two from a previous relationship. He's a bit of a bad boy, sure, quick to anger, always insists on things being done exactly as he's decided, but at the same time that's his strength: He knows what he wants, he's an adventurer, a conqueror. You try to soothe his temper without quite knowing how. Your eldest daughter is difficult. She has never accepted her parents' separation, being taken away from her father. Her relationship with this new man is explosive, there are fights and standoffs, the whole family bears the brunt. After she leaves home for university, life instantly seems calmer, more joyous. In the summertime you and your partner take groups hiking in the mountains. You go back to school.

Then one summer afternoon when she is back for vacation, staying with friends in a neighboring village, the eldest daughter, who has never once set foot in the house since she left, tells you this.

Twenty years later I reread Carrère's book. I try to read it the way my mother would have read it at the time, and also the way I would have read it then. It's complicated. I get caught up reading it through my eyes today. The book is an attempt to expose and analyze the subtle forces and positions in power relationships that are not always clear.

I dare say there aren't that many ways of speaking to someone who has killed his wife, his children, his parents, and lives on after them. But I realize with hindsight that I immediately rubbed him the right way by adopting that tone of pathetic and sympathetic gravity and by seeing him not as someone who had done something horrific but as someone to whom some horrific thing has happened, the unfortunate toy of diabolic forces.

This disconcertingly pertinent observation indicates the power that the perpetrator might not even be aware that he has over his victim, may not be conscious of wielding, convinced as he is that he's caught up in a spiral, a tragic destiny that exceeds him. It's what my stepfather told himself. He might still be saying it to this day as a way of validating the fact that he has successfully rebuilt his life. Something happened. Something happened to us, to him and to me, but mostly to him because I never really existed in his private belief system.

And what did I tell myself? What do the little victims tell themselves?

1) If you don't tell anyone, it's not real. As long as no one knows, it's not real.

2) You must have done something to deserve it. Something about you provoked him. You're a little whore.

3) You're his favorite. He does it to you because he loves you. He chose you. In her podcast, Charlotte Pudlowski talks to a woman who as child was abused by her grandfather, and who describes her feeling of betrayal when she discovered he was abusing other little girls. She thought she was the only one.

I felt a sense of betrayal too, for a slightly different reason, when I found out during the trial that he'd had mistresses. He'd never told me, though he had told me lots of other things. He used to say he told me everything, unmentionable things, that he confided in me in a way he had never done with anyone else. He knew I would never tell anyone. There was an intense intimacy between us, an intimacy known only to victims and their abusers. So I was surprised to find out he'd lied to me about his mistresses. I'd always thought that at least I had that, the truth. But no, I didn't have anything.

4) It's an ordeal. Get through it and you'll be able to do anything.

I'm already quite far into writing this book when it occurs to me to try and get hold of the legal brief. I want to compare what I'm describing with what is in the dossier—the things I said at the time, the evidence he gave, the psychiatric reports. It's not that I think that what's contained in the documents holds more truth than my own memories, but it seems an interesting idea to compare them.

I ask my mother to send me the dossier. She tells me it's been lost. I'd left France before the trial. I'd got a job as a teaching assistant at an American university as part of an exchange program, and I left. In America I had a series of short-term job contracts and lived a nomadic lifestyle. My mother moved house several times as well. But what does it matter if it's lost? There's no point nourishing an obsession with the past if you can't change anything.

If the documents were really so important to me, I should have held on to them. If they've got lost, it's also because I let it happen.

I set about trying to find out if somewhere there's a copy.

I email the woman who was my attorney at the time. It was my mother who'd found her. I think she wanted a woman to represent us. It was a good idea. The attorney was young and pretty. She had presence, which my mother and I did not, and in a way she bestowed it on us, enabling us to convey what we had to say so that our words were not rendered unintelligible by the shame that fettered our mouths.

She writes back to tell me she kept a copy of the file for ten years and then destroyed it. She suggests I contact the regional archives in the Hautes-Alpes department, who in turn refer me to the *tribunal de grande instance*, the regional court, in the city of Gap, who do not respond.

I decide it might be interesting to have my lawyer's perspective on the case. I'm not sure why I am looking for alternative points of view at this particular point in my investigation. Am I chasing my tail? Am I afraid of my univocal version? I have the feeling that I'm in danger of losing myself in the quest for a truth I've been seeking for so long, whose fleeting nature I am all too familiar with, but that I can never quite reach.

I ask if she would be prepared to talk to me over the

phone and she agrees immediately. She's a very busy person. I look her up online and see that she's part of a group of activists fighting for migrants' rights, a controversial topic in the Hautes-Alpes. I know a few other people involved in such groups who've told me how draining it is. Every day ever-increasing numbers of refugees arrive in Briançon and there's nowhere to accommodate them. The temporary shelters are filled to overflowing and there is a simmering threat of violence.

She takes time out of her hectic schedule to talk to me for a full hour about a case that took place twenty years earlier, and she doesn't even have any documents to refer to. I'm astonished at the clarity of her recall. She remembers my mother coming to ask her to represent me, me showing up to see her sometime later, on my own, my brother and sisters, the trial, and him of course, the defendant, the rapist.

He's the one she remembers the best. She was very struck by him. By him, by me, by the gravity of the affair. She remembers how hard it was to draft her plea statement because there were no witnesses, just a gaping silence around the crime that no one had had any inkling of until I had told my mother. She remembers certain horrible details, a room in the basement, the abuse that took place while my mother was at work that went on for a very long time, from when I was eight or nine until after I'd gone through puberty. And even a little after that, she says, when for fear of me falling pregnant he used to sodomize me. I finally decided to speak up when my youngest sister was the age I had been when the abuse started. I told myself I would never forgive myself if he subjected her to what he did to me. My mother spent a whole year in such shock she couldn't bring herself to leave him. The only solution was to press charges, to get him away from the little ones, to force her to leave him.

She remembers his charisma and his odd quirks of character, how egotistical he was, not uncommon in men with a certain status in the mountaineering world. She remembers him doing rock climbing and working in what used to be called acrobatic labor, where laborers on dangerous construction sites are roped together for safety. She had a friend who owned a construction company in the south of France who'd given him work. She conjures a portrait of an attractive, strong, controlling man who couldn't bear anyone standing up to him. She found his explanation of why it had happened completely mad: He claimed he could not bear being rejected by a little girl, and that the only way he could get close to me was through sex. It was a ludicrous explanation: How could a little girl love someone who raped her? But he clung to this version. She remembers the fetishism, the pleasure he took in completely possessing someone. How I became his object.

She remembers me too, both the young woman of twenty-one and the little girl she pictured while I was giving evidence, my fierce determination not to let him get to me. Dissociation had been a conscious means of survival for me—he wasn't doing it to me but to an object of his desire—and now it allowed me to articulate what he had done. I withdrew, put myself out of reach. She had represented other victims in similar cases, often they had fallen apart, had been utterly destroyed by what had happened to them. She remembers I had done well in high school and won a place at a *grande école*, one of France's highly selective elite universities. According to her I had a breakdown after the trial and quit school, as if my resistance had reached its limit with my allegations.

Some of the details she recalls don't correspond to my memories. I want to correct her, as if my version must be the right version. My mother also wants to correct things when she spots something in my account that is slightly unclear. It takes some fine-tuning on both sides to arrive at a version we all agree on. Verify dates, places, specific circumstances. One more time. When exhaustion takes hold, I wonder why it matters. I know it matters, but there are times I just don't care anymore.

There is the question of age, which you might be wondering about too. Was I seven, eight or nine? Did it go on until I was fourteen, or longer? There are incoherencies in the account. Incoherencies are dangerous, they call into question the reliability of the person who is speaking, you start by doubting one detail and end up doubting everything. When I filed the complaint with the police I was asked for precise dates, but I couldn't be more than approximate. I said I was about nine because I had lots of memories of the basement where we were living then. Delving back into my memories I managed to piece together episodes that had taken place quite a bit earlier. When I described memories to my mother from the time before we lived in the basement, I saw her crumple. I'm not surprised, she said eventually. That would explain the safety pin. I didn't know what she was talking about, so she told me how once, in the early days of our life with him, I had stuck a safety pin into my vagina, which she'd had to remove. I would have been six or seven. My step-father confirmed pretty much everything I said but he never volunteered anything. He was never prepared to say exactly when it had begun, or to describe the first time. He said he didn't remember. It was quite normal that I didn't know, I was seven, or eight, or nine years old. But he was twenty-five, or twenty-six, or twenty-seven. How could he have forgotten when it began?

At the end of the conversation, I ask the lawyer if she thinks things have changed. She tells me that nowadays, relative to twenty years ago, the words of the victim are taken much more seriously. It's not that there is more or less sexual abuse than there used to be, but there are more accusations. Even so, cases often end up being dismissed for lack of evidence. It is the victim's word against that of the accused. In my case this wasn't an issue because he confessed. She acknowledges that this doesn't often happen, and probably if he hadn't con-fessed, if he'd accused me of lying, he wouldn't have been found guilty.

He acknowledged his guilt right up until sentencing. But then, toward the end, as the prospect of prison loomed, he began trying to defend himself, claiming extenuating circumstances and concealing certain facts. He was pre-pared to recognize his guilt, but he didn't want to be punished too harshly, he said he deserved to be reinte-grated into society, he promised he would never do such a thing again, he was a man of his word.

Multiple witnesses took the stand during the trial to speak in his defense. None contested the crime, but all spoke of his qualities, they said he was a man of consummate integrity and loyalty, a fine son, a faithful friend, a tireless worker, intrepid, even at times heroic, when it came to rescuing someone in the mountains or in some other kind of danger. I can't help wondering what they think of themselves today, twenty years on, if they ever cast their minds back to the testimony they once gave in defense of a man who had raped a child. They had nothing to gain by supporting him, they did it by choice, in good conscience, they must have considered it perfectly rational to turn up at the courtroom to testify in this man's defense. Among them were a friend of my parents, a guy I liked, who'd worked with him on major construction sites, repairing a dam in the Alps and building the dome of the Lyon opera house; various women who visited him in jail; members of his family. They gave evidence about different periods of his life, from when he was young up until the trial (he was forty-one), each as irreproachable as the next. The crime was an anomaly.

Strangely, for me it's the opposite. His crime makes every other aspect of his life an aberration, renders it impossible to perceive anything about it through the prism of decency or any moral quality. Anyway, they were all exaggerating a little, these character witnesses, because they knew how domineering he was, how he never accepted anyone standing up to him; they all said he was controlling, but the way they said it made it sound like a virtue, a sign that he was strong-minded, a man of conviction. It's true that none of them had witnessed what we had seen at home, my mother and the children, the way he behaved like a tyrant. And yet that's what really comes through: a person who cannot tolerate any contradiction, who has to be in control of everything, who decrees, monitors, punishes, and never concedes authority.

Everything in the world is about sex except sex. Sex is about power. I'm not convinced this aphorism (attributed to Oscar Wilde) can be applied in every situation, but in the context of sexual violence I think it's spot on. Of course, sexual violence is about sex, but it's about sex as an instrument of control more than anything else. Children know this, even if they can't express it. *It wasn't sex*, says Bone, the little girl who narrates Dorothy Allison's *Bastard out of Carolina*, of what her stepfather did to her. *Not like a man and a woman pushing their naked bodies into each other, but then, it was something like sex, something powerful and frightening that he wanted badly and I didn't understand at all.*

When my stepfather was asked the reason for what he did, he said he'd been forced into the situation because he couldn't find any other way to connect with me. Seen from today, so long after it happened, that obviously makes no sense, but even then it didn't make sense to me. It was a clear admission of an abuse whose purpose was not simply sexual domination but something far beyond. Through domination and torture, an attack on life itself.

In April 2021 *Le Monde* published an article about a therapy center for sexual delinquents, in which the deep-seated motivation of the predator is described as *an attempt at a defensive solution to major anxieties linked to fundamental deficiencies, to prevent the risk of a depressive collapse.* According to Gaëlle Saint-Jalmes, a psychologist at the center with a long-standing interest in the ontology of violence, rape is a *psychological valve*: The abuser deploys sexual violence as a buffer against something even more terrible in himself. Society tolerates violence as a form of male self-defense, which probably explains why there are statistically so many more male than female rapists, and why male power, both physical and psychological, plays such a central role.

I can see my stepfather in this portrayal. He was fighting back, protecting himself. He sincerely believed himself to be the victim, not only of whatever social and human injustices he perceived in his life, but specifically in his relationship with me, because I hadn't wanted anything to do with him. He couldn't tolerate being rejected by a little girl to whom he was offering everything. She inflicted an intolerable narcissistic wound to his ego. Rape was a necessary punishment, to teach me to obey. And he turned up the radio to sing along with Johnny Hallyday, believing the lyrics from the depths of his soul:

> *I promise you salt in the kiss from my mouth*
> *I promise you honey with the touch of my hand*
> *I promise you the sky over your bed*
> *Flowers and lace to sweeten your nights*

Poor Johnny must be lying in his rococo mausoleum wondering how on earth he ended up in this book. Well, he can't blame me. I didn't choose the soundtrack.

He said he tried to talk about it, or at least to get people around him to realize that something wasn't right.

We were allowed to dress up for the end-of-year school fair. The children always went in costume, and sometimes the adults did too. One year my stepfather came in a very strange getup. He had managed to get hold of some brown coveralls. He must have gone to a lot of trouble, brown coveralls aren't exactly a dime a dozen, they're usually blue or gray, but he found some, pulled them on, fastened a length of twine that went through a roll of toilet paper around his neck like an enormous necklace, and wore a plastic toilet seat around his waist held up with some cord looped over his shoulders like suspenders. People were a bit surprised, not quite sure they got the joke.

—What are you meant to be?

—Guess.

—I'm not sure.

—Can't you see? This is a toilet bowl, and I'm a poo.

It was a bit too cryptic. He didn't elaborate, couldn't explain beyond this carnivalesque joke what it was that made him a shit in real life. But he seemed to think that with this costume he had sent out an SOS. He brought it up during his cross-examination to back up his claim that he'd tried to talk about it but no one had wanted to listen. He blamed my mother: Don't you remember when I dressed up as a shit? No one asked me anything! No one stopped to wonder why I thought I was a shit! Nobody, not even you!

I went along as a princess or a fairy or something.

I've written about it before. I look for the document on my computer. It was nearly twenty years ago. I'm repeating myself. I've been going round in circles, obsessing over the same thoughts and ideas for such a long time. Is it a consequence of trauma, to be doing this all the time? I don't know, I've never been in analysis or therapy. I've done nothing. I don't think it is to do with trauma, it's just life. Eventually I find the text, it's not an account as such, it's a poem called "Carnival," and it ends like this:

> Dressed up as shit
> He takes the princess's hand
> She doesn't want to give it to him
> But he grabs it
> He knows
> The little hand
> The shit he is
> Looks at it
> She watches from a distance
> Look at me
> The little princess
> Bathed in her light
> In her torn dress
> Looks, because she has to,
> But she says nothing
> He wants to be forgiven
> Somewhere within him someone wants to be forgiven
> She has no pity
> The queen of the ball in her torn clothes
> She gives him her hand because she has to
> But she does not want
> To forgive.

My friend Edmond illustrated the poem for a collection that was never published. Another project that never saw the light of day. The illustration dates back twenty years or so as well. Everything I have ever had to say about what happened to me is here: I'm in the foreground, wearing a costume that cannot possibly, given my macabre expression, make me look cute or funny. Behind me, against a storm-dark background, a beast like a whale is swimming toward me as though about to gobble me up. There's a stray dog in the corner that appears in almost all the drawings in the collection, a phantom presence linking one poem to the next. It's a Mexican street dog, skinny and hairless, with menacing eyes.

In my mother's laundry room, inside a plastic crate labeled with a sticker with my name on it in felt-tip pen, among a jumble of documents, letters, photos, and broken charm bracelets, the transcript of the court proceedings, issued by the High Court of Grenoble and dated June 2000, materializes at last. Within its pages, in clear and precise legal language, is everything I said during the trial about what had happened. There's a condensed biography of the accused, a summary of my testimony and that of my mother, and of my stepfather's statements. Again, his childhood in Paris, his youth in the Alps, the first time he met my mother, the abuse, his justifications. Most of his statements tally more or less with my version of what happened. It occurs to me I might include the document here. The juxtaposition of my prose with the legal language of the trial could make an interesting parallel, offering a means to compare two ways of writing about the same event and to tease out the differences.

> *Whereas, as to form, the proceedings are free of any nullity prejudicial to the interests of the parties; [. . .]*
>
> *Whereas, on the merits, the information as a whole has established the following facts: [. . .]*
>
> *Whereas the proceedings are complete;*
>
> *Whereas the investigation has produced sufficient evidence against . . . : [. . .]*
>
> *Having regard to articles 199, 214, 216 and 802 of the Code of Criminal Procedure;*
>
> *For these reasons The Court*
>
> *Indictment Division sitting in chambers,*
>
> *Having deliberated in accordance with the law; Finds that [. . .] has been indicted*
>
> *And refers him to the Assize Court of the Hautes-Alpes department to be tried in accordance with the law for the crime of rape and the related offences of sexual assault referred to above.*

But what strikes me more than the similarities between the two versions of the facts are the slight discrepancies. Perhaps that explains why I felt the need to go through all the archives, to try and find some piece of the story that I haven't already turned over in my mind a thousand times. Again, this idea of finding another point of view. Is it about being more accurate? An attempt to fill in the gaps? Or is it a way of trying to extricate myself, to escape this subjective version that haunts and suffocates me?

For example: *He ended it the day Neige told him that when they had sexual relations she was not there, it was another person who was being assaulted.*

Reading this, I remember how odd I'd found this statement in the courtroom, his description of the epiphany: One day we were talking yet again about what he did to me, I told him he could carry on, I didn't care, he might as well have been doing it all to someone else. That was the moment, he claimed, that he began to be afraid he was going to disturb my mental equilibrium and damage me permanently. That was what made him stop. Apart from the obvious absurdity of the assertion, which implied that up until then it had never occurred to him that he was harming me, what is so strange is that I have a very detailed recollection of the negotiations that led to him ending the abuse, and the issue of my mental dissociation had nothing to do with it.

The thing is, I remember the conversation, I remember analyzing our relationship, telling him what I thought, facing him down: No, we do not have a special bond, you think you can get close to me, but it's not me, it's just my body. I don't recall where we were. It could have been in bed, in my room, in a car. He liked to talk after having sex. I had no choice but to listen, staring out of the window, or up at the ceiling, or at the pattern on the wallpaper. Sometimes, when he pushed me too far, I turned on him in fury. Written up in the trial proceedings, this conversation—which I would otherwise have completely forgotten—became an element of the case. It acquired a certain existence.

I also have the sense that in a way the transcript of the trial, stamped and sealed, with its articles of law, attorneys' and clerks' signatures, validates my story. It's not just that otherwise the reader might think I was slightly exaggerating or embroidering a bit to give more weight to my allegations. It's also because there is a natural force at work in these kinds of stories that could be compared to his friends' and relatives' denial. You can keep a certain distance with this sense that the narrative functions like fiction, it's a true story, but in the end it is still a story, and focusing on this aspect of the account, on the language, means you don't have to be constantly thinking about what the language refers to. Photos, documents, letters from the time, the court report, all function as proof that it happened, independently of what I might say or think about it. They are pieces of reality that cannot be reduced to interpretations. They don't necessarily guarantee the truthfulness or good faith of the person who is writing, but they assume some of the responsibility of carrying this reality across time. They become the fragile crutches of this testimony without witnesses.

He made me wear a dress to the wedding.

I think my mother wore pants. They both wore white, but she cropped her hair and wore pants. A little rebellion. I wasn't given a choice. He liked me to wear dresses. He wanted me to think I was pretty. The day of the wedding I tried to change out of my outfit, but he wasn't having it. So I was the one who wore a dress, not the bride.

I'm not sure exactly how old I was, my brother was still a baby, so I must have been ten or so. I have to ask my mother. She must remember what year they were married.

She has no idea I'm writing this book, I guess I'll have to tell her at some point. She doesn't know why I asked her for the photos. The performance art project I was working on with the friends who were also victims of abuse came to nothing in the end, partly because of the pandemic, partly because our enthusiasm waned considerably once we began to think about the consequences. We were seized by a kind of psychological inertia that sucked out all our energy. The idea had been to plaster the walls of the space with family photographs for visitors to look at as they listened to recordings of our confessions playing over each other like a Greek chorus. Look at me now, without my friends, without the collective to carry words that I wish were not so blunt, without photographs, without a compass, all alone on my drifting boat.

What will you do then, O stolen heart?

I've never been in therapy or analysis. I haven't talked about it with a professional. Where I come from, we don't do that, we're afraid, we know what awaits in the kinds of places available to us, public services staffed by overworked, often barely qualified practitioners, free walk-in clinics with waiting rooms filled with deadbeats and losers, the Skid Row of mental illness, where the chances are you'll end up seeing someone who's either completely snowed under or pretty much incompetent. But I did tell my best friend Marianne one rainy afternoon on our way home from high school, and then, after I left home, university friends and my boyfriend. They all listened and believed me. No one doubted what I told them. I was guided, given advice. I was surrounded by a great deal of love. It was clear from fairly early on that pressing charges was the only option.

Bizarrely, it was Edmond's idea. We were lovers before we became friends. He was thirty-five years older than me. Another irony, but I'm just here to tell you the facts. The great thing about writing nonfiction is you're allowed to disregard plausibility, to relate facts and sequences of events that seem contradictory or even impossible, but which the reader is obliged to trust because according to us, that's how it happened.

This charismatic fifty-four-year-old artist, going out with a girl of nineteen, who had a weakness for much younger women—who was, in his own way, a predator—was my principal ally in the journey toward justice. He talked about me to a psychiatrist friend of his who told him that was what I had to do, there was no other solution either for keeping my brother and sisters out of danger, or for when eventually I decided to try and piece myself back together.

The only solution. But is it a solution? And if so, for whom? Talking about it, going to the police, means blowing the family to bits. As soon as the words come out, multiple processes of social exclusion are triggered. Everyone wants to shield themselves from the blaze. Shame is contagious, swift to propagate. People turn their backs on you. Within the family, and outside it too. You find yourself with barely any allies, just your closest friends, the few for whom you matter more than the shame you might bring upon them. For sure, this is a consolation, but not everyone is ready to live their whole life in such solitude.

It happens in Nice, on the old port, in a pink, ocher, gray apartment building. The girlfriend with whom I share the attic apartment is out for the night, leaving me on my own. I have assignments to work on but I can't concentrate. I go down two floors, knock on the door, Edmond's at home, he's working on a painting he'd begun sketching out that morning. The peeling plaster walls of the apartment are covered in drawings, painted phrases, portraits of women. Bodies dancing, suns, birds. It's a kind of naïve, beautiful manifesto on art and life, telling stories I want to believe. We chat, he does most of the talking, we look at books, he goes over to the shelves to pick out some more, he touches my face and shoulders. He's not sure how to entertain me. A strange, intense current circulates in the room. He doesn't know what to do with me. He thinks I'm in love with him, that I've come to him in search of that kind of love. We kiss, then go upstairs to the mezzanine and make love. But when it's over there is a sense of disappointment in the air. He tries to understand. He wants to be sure about this love affair. I don't know what it's all about, but one thing's for sure, it's got nothing to do with love. He's too old. He's older than my parents, he's an old man. I'm cool with having sex, but I don't give a damn about love. We fight. So, what is this, the two of us? It's not anything, if we don't talk about it, if no one sees us, it's nothing, we don't need to know what it is. But what is it you want? You're being a pain in the ass, I don't want anything, leave me alone. I get dressed. I leave. I don't go back upstairs, I go out for a walk around the port.

It's dark and slightly chilly. I pull the collar of my jacket closed. I walk toward the lighthouse, I follow the route automatically, it's the one everyone takes at dusk because it's the best place to watch the sunset. But in the dark there's nothing interesting to see and it's not safe, it's where gangs meet, people go there to do drugs, perverts masturbate as they watch addicts shooting up behind a block of cement. I keep going. The sound of the waves is soothing. Edmond comes after me. He finds me on the jetty. We stand there in silence for a long time, listening to the waters crashing against the rocks below. I smoke a cigarette. He stopped smoking years ago, but he gives me a light.

I tell him about the rape. He shouldn't be there with me on the seawall. I have nothing to offer him, I'm not even twenty, and already a war machine has trampled me, if he gets too close he'll get a gobbet of hate-filled spittle in his face that isn't even meant for him. I shouldn't be there either. I have to get on with my studies, fall in love with a boy or a girl my own age, learn to live now that I'm free. I have no business being on the seawall at this time of night with an aging Casanova. But I tell him anyway, the same thing I told my girlfriends. Except that he is an adult, someone with agency in the real world, with distance and discernment, and when I tell him the same story he doesn't hear it the same way. He asks me to roll him a cigarette. He takes a drag and coughs, then smokes it to the end with real pleasure. He throws the butt into the dark waters of the port. Neither of us speaks. We are suddenly so tired, as if all the exhaustion in the world is collapsing onto us. I'm ashamed to have told him but it's too late, it's done. He wishes he could tell me there's no reason to feel ashamed. He takes my hand. He won't let go for twenty years.

It takes time for me to even imagine agreeing to Edmond's suggestion. For months I reject point-blank the idea of going to the police. What can the rotten system do for me? What does some stupid bourgeois shrink know about the lives of people like us? But gradually things begin to fall into place. I finally tell my mother. A whole year goes by after my revelation, during which we seem to be getting nowhere. Then one day we're on the phone together and we finally agree that we've reached a stalemate.

Me, aged twenty-one, standing in a phone booth on a busy street in Marseille, choking back my anger: This can't go on, you've got to leave him.

Her, aged forty-three, at home, choking back the fear of being caught plotting: I can't.

Me: It's been a whole year.

Her: I don't know how to do it.

Me: If there's no other way, I'm going to the police. And if you don't support me, I'll do it on my own.

In concrete terms, filing a complaint is incredibly easy. You just write a letter and send it to the public prosecutor. That's the first step. There will be many others that proceed from the first, but this is decisive. The letter can be short and simple. You don't have to write well, or type it out, or print it off the computer, or know the appropriate

Neige Sinno
52 rue Roger Brun
13 005 MARSEILLE

Monsieur le Procureur de la République,

Je porte plainte contre mon beau-père pour abus sexuels sur ma personne durant les années 1988 à 1991. J'ai aujourd'hui 21 ans, j'avais au début des faits aux environs de 9 ans.

Je porte plainte pour le préjudice physique et moral sur moi-même ainsi que pour tenter de mettre hors de danger mon frère et ma sœur qui vivent encore à ses côtés.

À Marseille, le 30 mars 1999,

Neige Sinno

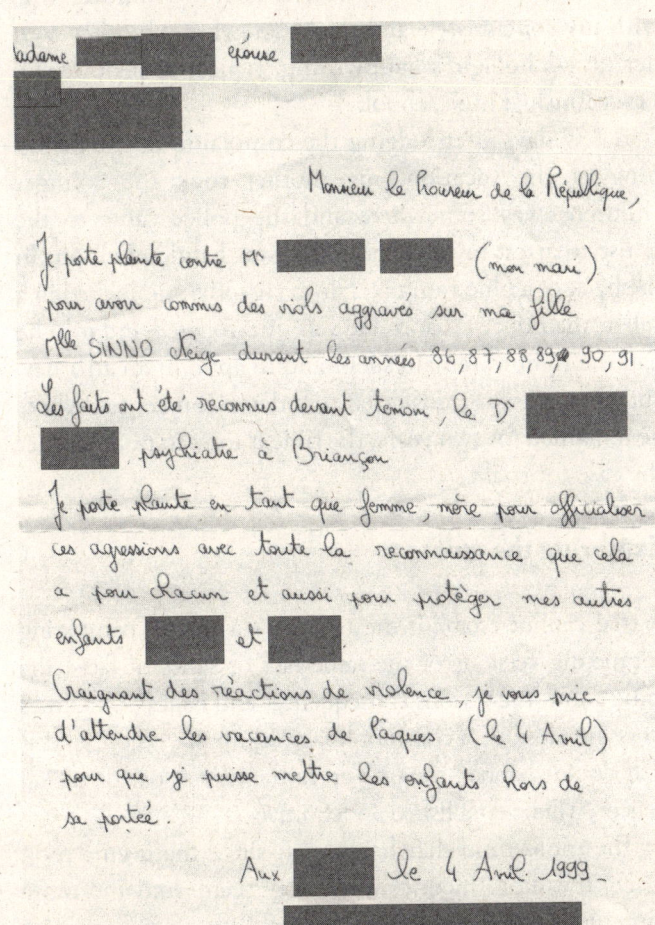

adame ▮▮▮ épouse ▮▮▮
▮▮▮

        Monsieur le Procureur de la République,

Je porte plainte contre Mr ▮▮▮ ▮▮▮ (mon mari)
pour avoir commis des viols aggravés sur ma fille
Mlle SINNO Neige durant les années 86, 87, 88, 89, 90, 91.
Les faits ont été reconnus devant témoin, le Dr ▮▮▮
▮▮▮ psychiatre à Briançon

Je porte plainte en tant que femme, mère pour officialiser
ces agressions avec toute la reconnaissance que cela
a pour chacun et aussi pour protéger mes autres
enfants ▮▮▮ et ▮▮▮
Craignant des réactions de violence, je vous prie
d'attendre les vacances de Pâques (le 4 Avril)
pour que je puisse mettre les enfants hors de
sa portée.

        Aux ▮▮▮ le 4 Avril 1999
        ▮▮▮

forms of address, or engage a lawyer. Just some words on a sheet of paper. It probably took us each five minutes. Me, with my concise style and messy scrawl, my mother with her neat schoolgirl's handwriting, typical of people who never finished high school.

A few days after lodging the complaint, at the beginning of the vacation, my mother took the younger children away somewhere and the police came to the house to arrest my stepfather. He was handcuffed, put in the back of a blue van, taken into custody, and locked in a cell at the police station. He was interrogated and told he had the right to remain silent and to appoint an attorney, and then he was transferred to a detention center, where he remained for two years, the time it took to put together the case for trial.

Exploring the gulf

A trial cannot establish the truth. It's a way of comparing competing versions of the same fact or series of facts, the same event, the various consequences and issues, sometimes to come close to a commonly agreed-upon version, and if that doesn't happen then it's up to the jury to decide which version will be established as definitive.

The more time that has passed since the events took place, the more inconceivable they seem, and the more difficult it is to count on the reliability of memory. It's ironic really, for despite the self-evident sketchiness of individual memory, traumatic memory is so deeply rooted it plays on a loop like a movie, appearing unwittingly in moments of abandon, in dreams. Yet this movie, which you find yourself plunged into quite involuntarily, doesn't necessarily portray what really happened.

That doesn't mean I'm not aware of the disjunction that Annie Ernaux evokes so beautifully in *A Girl's Story*, where the act of remembering becomes an exploration of *the gulf between the frightening reality of what happens, at the moment it happens, and the strange unreality, years later, of what happened.*

I experience this exact same sense of dislocation when I look back on different periods of my life, after I moved to Mexico, for example, I see myself in photos and wonder who that girl is, I try to piece together what she felt and experienced. I find myself able to describe my arrival from different angles, diffracting it to the point that it breaks into several distinct episodes. I have a strong memory of a blend of amazement and confusion, but I mix up the trips I took to villages in Chiapas and the desert. I remember the leather sandals I'm wearing in the photos, but it feels so distant, so detached from me, from the me that I am today, not exactly as if it's fictional, but almost.

And then when it comes to the rape it is quite the reverse, it's endlessly refreshed in my memory, it probably has been every single day since it happened, congealed in my brain, in the same form, always unchanging, a form in which sensations of hyperreality jostle with those of unreality as if they were a single sensation, the sensation of my entire being in revolt and which, by revolting against what cannot cease to be, annihilates itself.

For me, childhood remains a country of dark sunlit mornings, like in the poem by Alejandra Pizarnik:

I remember my childhood
When I was an old lady
Flowers died between my fingers
Because the wild dance of joy
Destroyed their hearts

I remember those dark sunlit mornings
when I was a child
it was yesterday
it was centuries ago

I remember places. Although I have a very poor visual memory, I can still remember details of the places. Sometimes even smells come back to me. I must have spent a lot of time not moving, looking about, while he did the things he did to me. Perhaps I fixated on external details as a way of trying to think about something else. Or maybe it was a collateral effect of dissociation, the part of me that dissociated from the body was free to wander without actually being able to escape, randomly recording things, bizarre decorative configurations, ornamental curiosities.

I remember the first apartment we lived in, the long corridor that led to the bathroom, the blue-green carpet that enables me to date the beginning of the abuse more precisely than when I first went to the police. I remember the basement of our next house, metal crates filled with mountaineering equipment piled on top of each other that he laid me down on. A large room that was being fixed up, him standing and waiting for me by the woodstove. Someone's spare room. A child's room at his brother's house. A mustard-colored counterpane with a fringe. A bedroom at my maternal grandmother's house, walls papered in bottle green. The basement of the ski store where he worked. I remember the smell of the ski wax. He was pretty brazen, a customer might have walked in at any moment. I was in the cross-country ski club. He took me to work with him, I'd fellate him, then he'd sort out my skis, and off I'd go with the instructor in the club's Citroën Méhari. Cars. Tents. A campsite. A chalet someone let him use. And every single room in the house, from the basement to the attic.

Apart from the scenes of rape I have almost no memories from back then. I can barely remember what I did at school, who my friends were, what we got up to in our free time. I've managed to piece some of it together from talking to my sister, but in my head it's vague and hazy, while the other things are unbelievably and horrifyingly precise.

And yet, with what degree of certainty can I say that what I remember is what really happened?

Gray area

During the trial it was extremely important to demonstrate that it was against my will. My lawyer remembers a discussion about pleasure and consent. It was obvious to me that I had never at any point consented, which my stepfather confirmed. On the other hand, he never stopped until I came. I remember concentrating to make it happen, or it would go on for an eternity. He took pleasure in giving me pleasure against my will. By giving me this pleasure he made me complicit in my own rape. Not only in his eyes, but in the eyes of the world. Maybe he thought it would work for me too, using orgasm as a smokescreen. But I knew, because I was living it, that an orgasm is not necessarily pleasure.

Even so, it does work sometimes. That's why for a long time Ludovic Degroote doubted the capacity of the word *rape* to describe what happened to him:

> when I read the newspaper I'm always reading stories about rape for thirty years I've wondered if my thing was also rape if it's the right word if deep down my responsibility for what happened doesn't forbid me from being a victim if I also took pleasure. . . .

Back in those days, people were very interested in the question of physical pleasure. Christine Angot talks about it in her books, how journalists were always curious to know if she had "taken pleasure," like in an interview she cites in *Le Voyage dans l'Est*.

> —. . . And from the point of view, without prying too much, but we're talking after all about such intimate things, at the same time, from the sexual point of view, was it only ever unpleasant? Or was there a mixture?
> —Are you talking about pleasure?
> —Yes.
> —Would you ask a battered child if they've been hurt? Why would you ask a child who's been raped if they experienced pleasure? A battered child is humiliated by blows, a sexually abused child is humiliated by fondling. Both are strategies of humiliation. Incest is a repudiation of parental responsibility, the child's subjection to

the service of the father's sexual satisfaction. Or another powerful person in the family. Knowing that they're being controlled, humiliated, degraded, that their life is being ruined, their future is in danger: what pleasure can a child take from that?

Not forgetting, of course, the issue of consent. A child who doesn't resist, doesn't run for help, doesn't stand up to their aggressor, scratch his face or something (obviously such images are absurd, no child is going to do that when it's their teacher, or brother or cousin or father touching them in a way that seems gentle, but let's suppose for a moment that it is possible)—does that mean they're consenting to what is being forced on them?

The thing that's hard to establish, even harder than the facts themselves, is what is meant by consent. Are we talking about what the child has done, or appears to have done, or felt, or appears to have felt, or what they said or failed to say? Laws that state clearly that there is no such thing as consent when we are talking about a child make things easier for everyone—including rapists themselves, who often try to convince themselves that the door was open and they were invited in.

Generally, I'm all for the existence of gray areas in life, blurred borders that permit excess, and are also thus the terrain of responsibility, choice, and free will. They are the territory of literature, philosophy, even science. So much of the adult world is made up of these gray areas, and the sharp angles of our triumphs and our setbacks are softened and eroded by the corrosive nature of this gray. But life for a child is black and white.

Even if it's not possible to say for sure if the door was wide open, might it be possible to claim it was slightly ajar? Light filtering through, like a signal to enter. Are you absolutely sure you didn't leave the door slightly open? Did you, whether inadvertently or through fear of some kind of retribution, fail to turn the key in the lock? How to be sure? The thing is, if it is decreed from the outset that there is no door, and thus it is not a question of whether the door was open or not, whether the door was forced or just needed a gentle push, that removes a significant amount of equivocation.

It's always wide open for a child. A child cannot open or close the door of consent. The handle is simply not within reach.

There's another document from the archives I'd have liked to include here. It's a collage of photos my mother made at the request of our lawyer in the days leading up to the trial. The case was put together in a rush, possibly because we were only given the date of the trial at the last minute, and I was in the US. Less than a week before the trial we were told we needed character witnesses. If there are no witnesses to speak for you, the lawyer explained to my mother, there will only be those speaking in favor of the accused, and they'll be given plenty of time to speak. And also, if the jurors see a radiant young woman of twenty-three in the witness stand, they won't be able to form a true picture of the situation, they'll keep thinking it's an adult making these accusations. We have to make them understand she was a minor. We need pictures of her at the age she was at the time of the abuse. You don't seem to grasp what's at stake here, the lawyer said, if you don't insist on the facts, and if your daughter keeps being so defiant about jail, there's a real chance he'll go free at the end of the trial, and the next week he'll be demanding joint custody of his two children. We were going to have to make a bit of an effort if we wanted to be heard.

We didn't have much choice when it came to witnesses. Marianne, the school friend I'd talked to about the rape before going to the police, agreed to testify. A friend of my mother's offered to speak on behalf of other friends and close family about their shock at the revelations, their deep remorse at not having spotted anything was wrong, and their commitment to supporting us. This act of bravery, along with putting up with being stuck in an anteroom for hours with the dozen or so witnesses who had come to speak on behalf of the accused, earned her my eternal gratitude.

My mother was in charge of the pictures. She'd always liked doing things with her hands, clipping pictures out of newspapers, sewing, crafting. She put together a collage of photos of me to circulate among the jurors. It wasn't sober, of course, sober is not her style. She didn't decorate it with colored tape or anything, but the piece of paper she chose to stick the pictures onto was fuchsia pink. It was very striking. If it hadn't gotten lost with the rest of the evidence, I'd have happily included it here.

We keep having to go back over the dates, the facts, the details, the photos of the little girl. There's always a danger of getting confused by this endless reiteration of the facts, the interminable interpretation. On top of doubts about the legitimacy of my allegations is the ambiguity of my so-called resilience. To the eyes of the jury and of the world, the fact that I'm doing okay exonerates my rapist. Even to my eyes. If he'd done something really terrible to me I wouldn't be where I am. I kept saying to myself, you're alive, your mind is functioning, you're free to leave, to think, to get on with your life. What have you got to complain about?

Model prisoner

The outcome of the case is not typical. In fact it's one of the rare examples of an accusation that is seen through to sentencing. First of all, most victims don't press charges: In France it's under 10 percent. Most cases end up being dismissed or disqualified. The most recent statistics indicate that 74 percent of all rape accusations, brought by both adults and minors, are dropped, and 50 percent of those that are investigated are requalified as lesser offenses of sexual assault or sexual abuse. Only 10 percent of cases end up in court, and there has been a drop of 40 percent in convictions over the last ten years. Ten percent of 10 percent is not a lot, that's one case out of every hundred, which means a low probability of conviction in the courts. Nonetheless, that is what happened in our case. My stepfather was handed down a nine-year jail sentence. Presumably this is because the rapes began when I was very young, went on for a long time, fulfilled the criteria of a serious crime, and were perpetrated by a figure of authority.

But it's primarily because he confessed and acknowledged the facts.

I don't know why he did it. If it had been my word against his, I'm sure I wouldn't have been believed.

So you could say that he helped me, in a way, and deserves credit for that. Was he seeking redemption? Forgiveness? I don't know. I don't think so, not my forgiveness anyway, which he never asked for. I think I stopped existing for him when I went to the police, perhaps I had only ever existed for him, in his world, his realm, as an object of desire, but stripped of any subjectivity. During the trial he continually referred to me, in my presence, in the third person. I don't know why he confessed. Should I be grateful? I don't think so. It just happened that way, for reasons entirely to do with him, one more decision I had no part in, my life irrelevant, again. But it's still true that if he'd denied it or lied, it would have turned out worse for me.

Among the papers I dug up in the storage crates while I was searching for the missing dossier, I found a letter he sent to my mother when he was first taken into custody. It's almost impossible to read now, because of the fax paper it was written or copied onto. It's incredible how everything about him is incised in me. His handwriting speaks to me as if I were hearing his voice. I recognize his way of forming the letters, how he exhales at the end of a sentence, the sound of his breathing, every last detail of him. I haven't seen him since the trial, twenty years ago, and yet even once when I watched a commercial he posted online I could picture him, that way he has of blinking nervously to disguise the unease behind his soft smile.

I copy out the letter word for word, changing only the names of my brother and sisters. I keep the spelling mistakes, the absence of the uppercase letter when he writes my name. This is not a rough draft written in haste. Everything he says in the letter is what he wanted to say. He wrote it on a sheet of fax paper and asked someone in the prison administration to mail it to my mother. He knew it was going to be read, would become an item archived in his case file, and if he had been allowed to speak in this book it's possible this would still be the way he chose to defend himself.

I type it out, insert it into the text, then delete it. In the letter he tells my mother how fed up he is of her endless lecturing and faultfinding, what he would like is to move forward together toward a greater well-being, for everyone, for he is suffering, he knows she is suffering too, the children are suffering. He knows he's going to go to prison, but from what he writes he seems to be thinking about after he gets out, about starting afresh with her and the children. He insists on being heard, understood. He explains that he never wanted to harm my mother's daughter, nor his own. Maybe he had wanted to hurt Sammy's daughter (but not to rape her, he adds, in brackets). What triggered his behavior was the refusal of the little girl to be his daughter, which she could have been if she'd wanted to.

I delete it because I can't bear it. The negation of the victim in what he writes is like a casual omission. He talks about the rape, calling it his *problem with neige* or *the neige situation.* He says none of it was my fault, I was just a catalyst, a spark. He insists, again, on his horror at the idea that he might ever do it to other children. It would be impossible for him to touch one of his own children, that would be utterly immoral.

I've heard it all before. When he used to unleash these arguments on me in person, with his magnetic personality and powers of persuasion, I accepted the logic. Written down it is much less convincing, absurd, flimsy. I sense that these are ideas that can't be put down on paper, they're machines that only function concretely in the dense obscurity of life. I used to hear an almost tragic dimension to his words. I felt so strongly the impossibility of loving him, a perception as hard and beautiful as the gleaming facets of a diamond. If I could have taken one step toward him, some kind of gesture of acceptance of his human kindness, he would have had no need to hurt me. But I didn't. I left him no choice.

The whole thing was utterly monstrous, I agree, but nonetheless I didn't want him to go to prison. Locking him up seemed out of proportion to the specific nature of the violence he'd subjected me to. I was also afraid that prison wouldn't change him.

The reason I hadn't wanted to press charges initially was because I was then—and am still—politically opposed to incarceration. Most of my friends at the time were students of literature and philosophy, or anarchist punks with pretty much the same reasons as me for being skeptical about the system. I'd read my Foucault. I believe prison alienates inmates and fails in its responsibility to rehabilitate them for when they are released back into society. It makes them more dangerous, by both destroying their affective bonds and turning them into victims, which only fuels their urge for narcissistic vengeance. The reason I spoke out about what had happened to me was because I wanted to protect my brother and my sisters. I asked my mother to take them away from my stepfather. Her immediate reaction was to ask him to see a psychiatrist. He agreed. For several months he saw someone in Briançon. I'll call him Plumage, because I am obliged to conceal his identity so he doesn't recognize himself, though as a doctor he adopted a position and should, in my opinion, own his responsibility for it. Dr. Plumage determined that this man posed no danger to children, he assured both my mother and me that there was no risk of him repeat offending, that pressing charges was not the solution. My stepfather stopped seeing him, got on with his life and with exercising his coercive control over us all. My mother asked for a divorce and he refused, claiming that he couldn't see the point, and explaining to her that divorce would be traumatic for the children.

We ended up going to the police because we couldn't figure out any other way of getting him away from us.

At the trial I said I was against the prison system, I didn't think locking him up would help him in any way, and it wouldn't help me either, it would simply add another layer of guilt to all the guilt I already bore. I asked for him to be prevented from having contact with us and made to undergo treatment.

But trials aren't about satisfying the victims. It's society that decides, through its representatives, what is right for it, not what is right for either the victim or the guilty party. He was sentenced to nine years in prison and to pay me compensation, but with no obligation to undergo treatment.

By the time of the trial he had already spent two years

in pretrial detention in Gap. After the sentencing he was sent to the Baumettes prison in Marseille. My brother and sister went to see him there. He asked them to bring him things, bars of chocolate, cookies, a pair of trainers. They felt uncomfortable doing that, as if he were asking them to do something illegal. But they did it anyway. They were obliged to visit him. It's the law. My mother tried to spare them the ordeal, but the judge threatened to take away her parental rights if she failed to fulfill her legal obligation: They were minors, and their father had the right to see them whether she liked it or not.

She drove them to the prison but didn't go inside. They were escorted in by people who volunteered at the prison. They were twelve and thirteen years old at the time of the arrest.

He was sentenced to nine years but served only five. Model prisoner, early release. It's classic for sexual delinquents. They are the rule followers of the prison system. My stepfather even managed to get himself transferred to a new experimental penitential center in Corsica, where inmates are free to wander at large in the nature reserve that surrounds the center. The prison is principally populated by male sex offenders convicted of child rape; they represent no danger either to the wardens or the other inmates, and after their release they are quietly reintegrated into society.

In 2017 Guillaume Massart made a documentary about this Corsican jail, *In the Open*. Casabianda, as the place is called, accommodates around 130 inmates, who live in a building that sits between the sea and an estate covered by some 1,500 hectares of forest. Most of them are there for intrafamilial sexual crimes. Clearly the idea is not that the establishment should be less harsh than a traditional prison, or that the child rapists housed there should receive favorable treatment. It is simply that they are obedient prisoners who will not try to escape, who are serving lengthy sentences and have time to devote to manual activities or working in the fields. You'd expect a significant amount of psychological treatment, different kinds of therapy, but there's not much on offer. It's basically just another carceral environment for punishment, not for cure. They are punished differently. The idea is that the gravity of their crimes and their shame weighs sufficiently heavily on them that they do not need anything more.

Massart did not set out to make a film about rapists. Initially his intention was to explore the penitentiary landscape, the issue of incarceration, the panopticon. He soon found himself invited into their cells because the inmates themselves wanted to talk to him. He considered how to position himself appropriately with regard to the prisoners. Not to distance them too much, but not to empathize with them either. The film goes back and forth in this uncertainty. Ultimately, he opts for empathy, specifically with one particular inmate, himself once a victim of child sexual abuse, who, during a walk in the woods, as the shadows of the branches flicker across his face, recounts in harrowing detail his past as a child prostitute.

In some of the interviews, Massart comes across as more forgiving than distant. He acknowledges that child molesters suffer the most ill-treatment within the traditional closed penitentiary system, where they are often beaten up and gang raped. No one listens to them or seems to care about their suffering. In this filmmaker they at last found a sympathetic ear to listen to what they have to say.

They have regrets. They would like to understand what they did, but aren't really able to talk about it, they're in denial. Though they are surrounded by other men deprived of their liberty for the same reasons, they don't talk about it with each other or feel any solidarity because of it. Though they work together and there's a certain conviviality in their everyday life, they don't constitute a community of penitents. Each man lives in his own infernal cage of solitude.

They're convinced they don't receive adequate support. They all seem to think they are the victims of grave injustice. No one tries to understand them. People are too quick to judge them, says one of the inmates, no one tries to understand how it came to this. They are ostracized from society, thought of as subhuman, as monsters who cannot change, but they are human beings, they have feelings, they suffer. They go on and on about themselves, about the indifference of which they are the victims.

I don't think it's true that society makes no effort to understand them. I think it's quite the opposite. There's a lot of focus on how and why it came to this. It is the secret center of our world, the unimaginable evil that is part of who we are. Think of our fascination with sensationalist headlines about such crimes.

I, in any case, have always wondered about these things. And when I see the images of these inmates staring sadly out to sea, their bodies bowed beneath the burden of their crimes even as they stroll toward a possible future, I see my rapist, the way he stands with his hands in his pockets. Again, I put myself in his shoes, I imagine what he's thinking, the responses he might have given to the filmmaker, when he was being sincere and when he was seeking external approval.

He'd never been able to sit peacefully looking out at the landscape, not moving, contemplative, but sometimes now when he walks along the beach he is astonished by the beauty. He thinks about his children. He's sorry they had to grow up without a father because of his wrongdoing. Does he think of me? Does he think about how I had to grow up without a childhood, without innocence, without illusions, because of his "wrongdoing"? It's possible the thought occasionally occurs to him, but it's so unbearable that he instinctively banishes it. He tells himself that I'm strong, I must surely have managed to make a fresh start. Or perhaps he doesn't tell himself anything, he's deleted me. Perhaps it's quite the opposite, he has memories of the pleasure he got from dominating me, that feeling of absolute control. Perhaps deep down he's proud of having dared to experience what so few people allow themselves to. He went to the absolute brink of desire, and now he accepts the consequences.

What is a monster, exactly, if not a being so abnormal he cannot be understood, he cannot even understand himself? Why aren't they monsters, these men who put their erect penises into the bodies of their own children as they whisper in their ears, in soft voices so no one can overhear, that they love them more than anything in the world? They don't want to be defined exclusively by these acts. Presumably they too, like my mother used to say, have good qualities. Once upon a time they too were innocent children, but their behavior as adults has transformed them into something else. And if that thing is not a monster, I do not know what is.

It's not easy, having been a victim, to watch a film like this that acknowledges the abuser's humanity. Their victims remain abstract, because they are absent, unseen. They are given no voice. They barely figure in the words of the inmates, who only want to talk about what they call their errors, their imprudence, one of them says it was a "stupid mistake." They claim to understand the gravity of what they have done, but they never actually talk about it. None of them admits to having repeatedly raped a child, sometimes for years, even though that's the reason they're in prison.

I suppose it's understandable that they can't face up to the gravity of their crimes. Were they able to, they would surely kill themselves. Which is in my opinion the only honorable exit for a child rapist. To die of shame. But no, they don't commit suicide—it is usually the victims of incest who kill themselves, not the perpetrators—they demand their right to a second chance. And we, society, having handed them long prison sentences, choose to believe they deserve that right, for one day the sentence comes to an end. Their debt has been paid. They can go free.

CHAPTER II

GHOSTS

(and then I see a darkness)
—Will Oldham

Thirty years later, some observations on trauma

One day I understood it was all over, the rape, my childhood, our family. I could go away and get on with my life. I thought then that I was free. But no one is ever completely free, because nothing is ever really over, and even if you become a different person, this sliver of darkness will follow you. He was gone. He couldn't hurt me anymore. I could go out into the world, meet people, talk, laugh, and he would never be able to touch me again. Except that everywhere I went, at any moment, I'd turn my head and glimpse his shadow.

Most people who aren't familiar with the issue probably think that the main impact of being repeatedly raped for years on end is on the victim's sexuality. They assume that those who have suffered it must struggle with problems in their relationships and their sex lives. Obviously, we do have these kinds of problems, but in reality they are often the least of our concerns. Rape, as we have seen, is primarily an issue of power rather than of sex, and if we don't take this into account, we can't properly understand the phenomenon. Nicolas Estano, a clinical psychologist who works as an expert witness at the Paris Court of Appeal, explains in *Le Monde*, that *rape, rather than being principally an expression of sexual desire, is a way of using sex to express anxiety around power and anger. It is a pseudo-sexual act, an ensemble of sexual behaviors that are more to do with status, hostility, control, and domination than with sensuality or sexual satisfaction.* In other words, sexual predation is less about physical pleasure than it is a relationship of domination, that is, power. The abuser chooses this kind of abuse because it is a means of subjugating the other that goes beyond other possible forms of control.

His power over me was absolute, it gave him the sensation while he was raping me that he was a superman. My life and death were in his hands. This monstrous identity, a label they all reject after the fact, gives them a deranged pleasure: A monster, once seen, is subhuman, but when no one can see him he is a king.

The notion of subjugation is helpful not only for understanding the abuser, as a way of explaining their motivation and the function of psychological release, but also for understanding the victim. A person who has been raped is above all a person who has for a time been wholly under the thumb of another person who wielded absolute power over them. Being sexually abused is a form of submission that impacts the very foundations of a person's being.

Sometimes I just wanted him to stop holding back and kill me, once and for all, put an end to the whole thing. Once I understood that there was a way out, something lit up in me. The revelation that I could only bear so much, that if I wanted to I could die, has been a great help to me ever since. That day, when I wanted to die, I suppose I did die a little, and it is the ghost who survived me who has been able to hold herself together to this day. The part of me that couldn't hold it together has gone where she had to go, the other part, the part that wanted to stay, is me. But the split isn't so simple, we are constantly thinking about each other. She hasn't gone far, that cursed part of me, I hear her often, her ragged breath, the catch in her voice, I see her reflection in the mirror, she slips into my sleep. She is always there, waiting, for I do not know what.

The consequences of rape go well beyond the specific realm of sex, affecting everything from one's ability to breathe to one's ability to talk to people, eat, wash, look at paintings, draw, speak or stay silent, perceive existence as reality, remember, learn, think, inhabit one's body and life, or simply feel able to be.

I do have a few anecdotes about sex though, I wouldn't want to disappoint anyone who considers sex to be a key factor, especially if they've read this far.

Like many men who commit incest, my stepfather often asked me to fellate him. It's something that can be done just about anywhere, makes no noise and leaves no trace. A lot of bang for your buck, you might say. It's an act that exemplifies the intense pleasure of absolute control. To insert the penis into the mouth of a child is to penetrate not only their body but also their mind. True, other types of assault also touch the mind, and the heart as well, but concretely and symbolically the penis in the mouth connotes absolute submission. It also obliges the victim to participate. Not only is it impossible to dissociate completely, as one can during acts inflicted on the sexual organs, for example—you have to take care that your teeth don't nick the tender skin of the penis, for example—but you're doing something, you're not passive, you can't just lie there and wait until it's over. That's no doubt a slightly simplistic explanation for the recurrence of fellatio in the sex acts demanded of children, though I'm sure there are plenty of other insightful explanations. Over the years, obviously without setting out to, I became a seasoned practitioner. I always swallowed. It was part of the process, and I never questioned it. For a long time afterward, even once I was free to do as I pleased, I continued systematically swallowing.

One day it occurred to me that I could spit. I think I was over thirty by the time I realized this. It was a revelation, a small epiphany. I became conscious of the fact that I was always repeating an aspect of the rape, and what's more that I didn't particularly like giving blow jobs, I did it without really thinking of my partner's pleasure, I'd conjure up mental distractions, not actually dissociating but nonetheless somehow kind of absenting myself. Spitting was a way of confirming that I was free to do as I pleased. It opened a small window of variation that transformed the way I gave blow jobs. I began to take genuine pleasure in the act, playing with different movements and strokes. Most importantly I learned to anticipate with a certain impatience the moment I could spit into my hand the viscous fluid that no one was going to force me to swallow. It's a delight every time, an intense joy, a joy that doesn't need to manifest, though I imagine a faint, mischievous, slightly crazed smile must sometimes show on my face and vaguely intrigue my partner.

It's in that same spirit that I prefer to tell the truth. I don't mean that the relationship between spitting and telling is in both cases about expelling something toxic from the body. What I mean is that I like to tell the truth even when a little white lie would be welcome. Just like spitting, I like the sense that this gesture grounds me in my freedom to choose. I was forced to lie for so many years. I didn't have a choice. Now, even if sometimes there are serious consequences and it isn't worth it, I tell the truth with aplomb and pleasure.

I hope the word blow job doesn't shock you. One of my friends felt that driving it home with such language was a way to bludgeon the reader into facing up to the horror of the act, as if otherwise they might not truly understand. That is not at all my intention. Again, language alters when it shifts from one sphere to another. In the sphere of trauma, the words that my abuser used have become taboo for me, tainted by shame. It's pure chance. He used the words "sex," "lick," "suck," "touch," "cock." He said I was "pretty" or "cute." He gave me "cuddles." I can't bring myself to use these words anymore, I find them excruciating, and I haven't attempted to reintroduce them into my vocabulary, or to give them a new life by associating them with different things. I've simply eliminated them.

But I have no problem with the word *pipe*, the French for blow job. I love this word, it's funny, it always makes me stop and think: what's the link between fellatio and a pipe? No idea. I don't find it vulgar, in a way it's a bit of an intellectual word: Think of the painting by Magritte with its subtitle interrogating the notion of representation (*ceci n'est pas une pipe*: this is not a pipe). It's the same with the English word blow job. It's a completely different word to *pipe*, two little words stuck together that don't really have anything to do with each other. I mean, if there's one thing you don't do, it's blow, right? We're not blowing, and it's not (at least it's not supposed to be) a job; as is often the case, we're doing something completely other than what we seem to be doing, made all the more obvious by the almost comically untechnical words used to describe it.

There's a lot of talk nowadays about a more progressive view of sex in which penetration is not necessarily the goal. People who rape children already know this. Rape is linked in both our imagination and the law with the image of forced and violent penetration, but child rapists often avoid it, sticking to other acts that allow them to convince themselves that what they're doing isn't really rape, sexual abuse isn't so bad, and it also keeps their victim in a state of uncertainty that thwarts any attempt to find the words to speak.

I remember how impatient I was for it to happen. I was curious, I wanted to know what it felt like, and also it would confirm that what he was doing to me was rape. Up until then I wasn't sure. He waited a long time, until a moment that just about corresponded with a certain awakening of my awareness. I was about twelve. I remember the joy that accompanied the act. At least now I was sure that it was what it was.

Because I was raped

It took me a long time to learn to appreciate normal or superficial relationships with people. In both friendships and romantic relationships, even at parties or when I hitched a ride with a stranger, I always found myself seeking a greater degree of intensity, a dimension where the breezy nature of normal conversation no longer applied. That was the space in which I had learned to function, and anything else seemed vapid. Torture creates a bubble of intimacy where you only truly exist in the eyes of the other, and the other only exists, in the most truly authentic way, in your eyes. Or at least that's what you think, that's what the state of nakedness in which you find yourself makes you believe. Like a drug, being plunged into an extreme situation gives you the sensation of living more intensely. The sensation of absolute truth. It's not true, obviously, but it is not easy to undo a perception that all your senses, your entire being, have hitherto always experienced as incomparable.

A central problem for a survivor of sexual abuse is that of self-image. The child who is raped becomes, like everyone does at adolescence and then at adulthood, a narcissist, but a warped narcissist who looks at their reflection and sees a hideous monster, a deformed body, an ugly face. No, not ugly. Nor deformed. Something else. We look at ourselves in the mirror and see what our rapist sees.

A desirable body. Neither beautiful nor ugly, but something about it provokes desire, awakens unwholesome appetites. A body that is too beautiful or too ugly, it's irresistible, by which I mean it is monstrous, disgusting, a body and face with malign properties that irrepressibly attract not contemplation or admiration or tenderness, but the need to seize them and, in every way possible, defile and destroy them.

You can't escape the mirror. I remember as a child looking at myself with morbid curiosity. After a while I'd experience a sort of vertigo, as though I could see conflicting internal responses to my reflection happening simultaneously. You know you'll get hurt in the process, but you can't keep yourself from looking because it's fascinating too.

I still experience this unsettling dissonance in the changing room when I'm shopping for clothes. Like a yogi, I have learned to let these thoughts and sensations pass through me as though they were products of (part of) my mind, and I let them do their thing, while trying not to get too upset. I usually end up in tears, but I know it will pass. I look at myself and the sight of my body makes me cry. My reflection in the mirror confirms that I have a body, that I exist as a body, I'm not just a brave little brain or an eye looking intently at the outside and the inside with innocent curiosity. This uncomfortable recognition is overlaid onto the perception of the uniqueness of this body, I have only one, it has its borders, borders that I cannot control. It is neither beautiful nor ugly, but I hate it.

Alternating between provocative clothes and oversize sweaters that conceal the body, between sexy lingerie and clogs, trying to understand the logic of attraction and repulsion, which is impossible to understand because it's always shifting, and these shifts aren't in tune with the thinking entity that looks, analyzes and constructs judgments based on what it sees. I hate buying clothes. The changing room is an ordeal. But I also hate being badly dressed.

How I would love to be at ease in clothes. As Virginia Woolf wrote, ah, the unknown joy of walking around cheerfully in a new dress!

> The looking glass shame has lasted all my life, long after the tomboy phase was over. . . . Everything to do with dress—to be fitted, to come into a room wearing a new dress—still frightens me; at least makes me shy, self-conscious, uncomfortable. "Oh, to be able to run, like Julian Morrell, all over the garden in a new dress," I thought not many years ago at Garsington; when Julian opened a parcel and put on a new dress and scampered round and round like a hare.

For a long time, certain words inspired feelings of disgust in me. I could never say the word *viol*, the French for rape. Which is paradoxical, for it's the word that freed me: I remember that once I could put a name to what was happening to me I felt it like a current of cool air flowing through me. But there was a period of adjustment. There were even words that have nothing to do with *viol*, but because they contained the same two syllables, they triggered an instinctive repulsion: *violet, violin, ravioli*. Even now, I only have to hear these words for my body to tense up involuntarily. It's more muted than it used to be. Before, it was like a little electric shock. Now it's more abstract, a fleeting sensation of unease.

For a long time, many things made me nauseous. Food, stubble, sweat. The physical reaction has grown less pronounced, but I still have an aversion to specific smells, textures, ways of speaking, movements.

There are the nightmares of course, but now they usually fade after a few hours, a few days for the most persistent.

When it comes down to it, none of this seems so terrible. It's not much at all really, the odd bout of nausea, tiny mortifications and small victories. It's a normal network of obsessions, everyone has them. Those of people who have been raped are to do with rape, which seems logical. The problem for me was that for a long time, whether I liked it or not, whether I chose to stifle it or shout it from the rooftops, I saw everything through the lens of rape. It's still the case today: Even though now there are lulls when I can think about other things, even though it's not always about that, often it still is. In that sense he won and there's nothing I can do about it. *Damaged for life.*

Whenever I'm asked to name my greatest strength, the strength that defines me, I say I'm brave. I say it almost without thinking, I don't even know if it's something I'm proud of. I say it because I think it's true. That is my strength. The midwife who assisted when I gave birth—who wasn't what one would call overflowing with compliments—told me I was brave, and she'd attended quite a few births in her time. She was seventy at least and had lost two young children of her own, but in that shared moment of terror and grace, as death brushed close to us, to me and her and Max and our baby who didn't yet have a name, she looked me in the eye and saw what was there: Fear, grief, anger, hope, a thousand things, but what she saw most of all was immense courage, a force both cruel and innocent, almost obscene in its intensity, the desire to face the darkness.

It's not dissimilar to what the lawyer meant when she spoke of my unbelievable determination to get this man out of my life, and the strength I put into moving on. He didn't make me brave. That was my response to the abuse. But still, that's where it comes from. The strength I draw on in moments of despair, when everything seems too much to bear, comes from what I experienced, from what he did to me.

He made my entire character. The good and the bad. The brilliant and the terrible.

I am all of these things, and everything stems from my childhood.

I struggle to believe I exist. I don't know how to protect my bodily space. I allow myself to be invaded by other people.

I have an inner life. A splendid, infinite, secret inner life that belongs only to me. I remember when I was little, I used to think that, given what my life was, being in prison wouldn't be hard at all, I could spend years locked in a cell and I'd still be able to live inside my head. I can be doing anything, and I'm always able to take a moment for myself to retreat into my private world.

I have a tendency to underplay my intellect for fear of annoying people more powerful than me, in case it unsettles them. In professional relationships I automatically position myself as subordinate.

I have a great capacity for dissociation. I can focus on something for hours and not lose my concentration, wherever I am, however noisy or busy the surroundings. I am entirely capable of mulling over a knotty translation problem in the middle of a techno rave.

I have a poor memory. I can't learn anything by heart, even a short poem. It's as though there is only room in my memory for either very precise memories that I can't control, or vague recollections that end up taking on a certain reality, a particular precision, despite the lack of detail of the event they refer to, from having been obsessively summoned.

I have a high pain threshold. I can completely ignore my body, my mind and my emotions. I can go an entire week without eating.

Sometimes I lose myself, fall into a black hole so deep I can't see the bottom. It takes a while to extricate myself.

I am drawn to and repelled by the subversive.

I am viscerally incapable of believing in anything spiritual. I have no faith. Anything to do with the soul leaves me at best indifferent, at worst filled with pity or distrust. That line from Nietzsche about art being the only thing that gives meaning to life seems to me to be absolutely true, and it also seems to suggest that beyond art nothing has meaning, everything is perfectly cruel and absurd.

I grew up in a lie. The lie made me. It's even linked to the discovery of myself as an individual. When I realized I had to lie, this lying *I* seemed to belong to me, to be me. I don't think I had ever been aware until then of the absolute loneliness that constitutes the core of every human being. I discovered my identity in the same exact moment in which dissimulation was imposed on me. My interior world was forged in my understanding of myself as a stranger in a world in which I could never reveal who I really was. The secret, and the fact of knowing that I survived it, was my strength. All it would have taken was a few words and I could have made my entire family fall apart. I figured this out pretty quickly. I remember getting so angry, and toying with the thought of what could happen. I have one very clear recollection: I'm washing dishes while my mom is drinking tea with a friend. I'm annoyed because they still make me wash the dishes, because I'm excluded from their grown-up conversation, because no one's paying me any attention and I'd like to be included. I'm scrubbing the plates furiously with a double-sided sponge and thinking about what I could say: He's been raping me ever since I was little. That's why I hate him. All he does is rape me.

It's going round and round in my head, getting louder and louder. HE KEEPS RAPING ME. I'm walking a tightrope between two cliffs, the world before I utter these words and the world after. HE RAPES ME. RAPES. RAPES. On one side life as we know it, on the other a new world that will begin with these words, the two women's reactions, and everything that follows. It would be horrible, that I know. It would mean real hardship. He'd have to leave, he'd go to jail. My mother left on her own with four children. We'd be sent to children's homes or foster parents. My brother and sisters wouldn't have happy childhoods. But I would have my brief moment of glory. One word would be all it took. RAPE. If my tongue stuttered on the word, the way in dreams your mouth turns into a disgusting paste when you try to scream, I could always howl it out, or trace it on the wall with the sponge. R. A. P. E. Four letters. And everything would change. But I say nothing. I finish the dishes. I say nothing, but I know I have the power. It scares me but I'm proud of it too. I know the family depends on me. I know my words can make things happen. And so can my silence. I'm filled with pride. I jealously guard my powers.

I idealize childhood, my father, people who are happy. I often think of the person I might have become if it hadn't happened.

I have an addictive personality, but there is nothing I am addicted to, I keep everything under strict, constant control. I ponder them, the addictions I don't have, magnanimously, and they sneer back at me.

I don't like it when people confide in me. But when they do, I never reveal a thing, I have never divulged anything that I've been asked to keep to myself. My silence is sacred.

He showed me his dark side, and mine, and that of the whole of humankind, and now when I cross paths with the damned, I look them in the eye and know we are the same. They get it; they know I have no moral right to judge them.

I know that truth does not dwell in language. I know that truth is nowhere. I know that talking about something can conjure up an experience that is not quite the same as the words describing it. Fiction has always been what interests me more than anything else in the world. I am fascinated by the phenomenon whereby what is being said is different from what is actually said. Where it is natural that what is said refers to an elsewhere, to a shadow of the language, where truth lurks but can never be spoken. It was my father, not him, who taught me to read. It was my father who gave me these weapons, imagination as a place of refuge, my taste for solitude. My love of literature was born of these revelations. But it was my stepfather who made me understand the duplicity of language and of silence. It is from that intimate understanding, that hate, that I write.

In reality it's got nothing to do with him as a person. In a variation on the words of April Ayers Lawson, it's *because I was raped*. Because I was raped. Because I was raped.

I'm interested in this use of the passive voice. Its significance resonates deeply within me. Passive grammatical construction makes the victim the object of an act committed by the subject, i.e. the rapist, as in the sentence my stepfather raped me. Whereas the words I was raped emphasize the act that is endured rather than the person who carries it out. At the same time, the subject of the sentence is me. The rapist has vanished from the statement. It describes a situation where something was done to me by an exterior force, it was impossible for me to act, my free will was suspended.

My stepfather also believed he was subject to forces stronger than he. He was crushed by these forces, he was *done to* and then he *did*, he saw himself as a tragic character, as tortured as Phaedra ceding to her desire for her stepson Hippolytus. Sometimes this is called compulsion. It's not so long ago that the inability to control one's emotional and sexual feelings was still known as passion, as in the legal term *crime passionnel*.

The inability to discipline human passion is a potent theme in literature. Passions are subversive; they fascinate because they threaten the social order. They are an affirmation of the strength of the individual rebelling against a society that seeks to suppress and crush them. These are the passions that one finds in Faulkner, irresistible impulses that we look upon helplessly, as if watching a flood or a storm. In the works of the Marquis de Sade, desire is a force of nature, indomitable, reflexive, beyond any notion of good and evil, because it is not a part of any system of ethics, it is a system of pure life. Are we responsible for the desires we feel if they are involuntary, if they act through us and not the other way around?

This was the way my stepfather talked about the rape, as something that had happened to him, to the two of us, rather than something he'd wanted or that he'd chosen to make happen. He was the victim, and somehow I was the executioner: me, the little girl who had set off the process simply by existing.

I don't want you to think I'm suggesting the victim bears any responsibility for being raped. In my mind, there is not a shred of doubt as to who is guilty. As I've said, killing himself seemed to me a more just resolution than years of incarceration. But when I was a child, he made me see it from his point of view, and even today I still understand him, albeit not in the same way, now that I have a certain distance. Would I be able to follow his reasoning if I hadn't at some point been at its heart? I don't know. In any case, what he meant was that there was nothing he could have done to resist his urge to rape me. I couldn't have done anything to fight back either. You'll say he could have talked to someone about it. Me too, I could have tried to get help. But the truth was, I couldn't. That is the strange nature of this tragedy: the inability to talk about it. Even if we'd wanted to, we couldn't. But let's suppose we were both subject by external forces to the same strange silence we were unable to overcome. Let's suppose that almost everything that happened, the rape, the inability to confide in anybody, the impossibility of resisting the urge to do it again and again and again, for weeks, for months, for years on end, is what happened to him. Let's suppose it was that, not rhetorically but in reality, after all it's quite possible that this does happen in some cases, probably not many, it's true, and even in those rare cases it's unlikely that there is at no point the possibility of choosing to act in a different way. But let's give him the benefit of the doubt.

If that were really the case, then this thing that happened to him, the abuse of a child he was supposed to protect, did change his life, had such a huge impact on his being that everything he has done since, even everything he did before, everything he will ever do or say or think from that point on, is linked to that event, that situation, that hell. The rape did it. And, if we follow this line of reasoning to its logical conclusion, I did it.

Every story of rape is unique. Every story of love or hate is based on something commonplace, but when it happens to you, it becomes unique. If he had committed a different rape, he would have been a different man, though he always swore he would never have done it to anyone else. He was deeply offended that anyone could intimate, as my mother and I did, that he might ever be tempted to touch my sisters and brother. He was outraged that he was given a prison sentence to protect possible future victims. He found the idea that there might be other victims inconceivable. He would never have laid a finger on a child born of his own flesh and blood. My sister Rose, just two years younger than me, who looks like me and lived in the same house, remembers him feeling her up, but it never went any further. It's something that happened to him and to me and it defines everything about us today.

The way of the tiger

A dead little girl says: I am the one who explodes with horror in the lungs of the living. Take me away from here right now.
—Antonin Artaud

You cart all this around with you, in different forms, for the whole of the rest of your life. In 2013, after several months of denial and alternative medicine, I agreed to have surgery to remove an ovarian cyst. Its proportions were so remarkable it could have been placed inside a jar of formalin and passed around a medical convention to impress astonished experts in the field. I wasn't in pain, which I'd decided was a good sign, and I'd been told that some ovarian cysts go away on their own. But between two sessions of acupuncture, psycho-corporal therapy, and various visits to the gynecologist, instead of vanishing by magic or even merely shrinking a bit as I'd hoped, the tumor had grown.

Eventually I took advantage of a trip to France to go and see a specialist. A doctor in Briançon sent me straight to the emergency room in Marseille and I was operated on a few weeks later. It turned out to be invasive ovarian cancer and I was going to have to throw myself into a series of treatments if I wanted to be saved. I was thirty-five.

At that point I hadn't read *Tiger, Tiger*, by Margaux Fragoso, published in 2011, the story of her relationship as a child with a kind, slightly eccentric neighbor who kept exotic animals, gave her the attention she wasn't getting from her family, and abused her for ten years. I'd read reviews that praised the book's literary qualities but wondered why readers would choose to immerse themselves in such atrocities, with detailed descriptions of rape, psychological manipulation, and the nauseatingly toxic relationship between the victim and her abuser, whose respective suffering came together to create a jail, a cage in which they were both trapped like tortured animals.

The title recalls "The Tyger," from William Blake's collection of poems, *Songs of Innocence and of Experience*, composed in London during the convulsive period of the French Revolution. With evocative verse and imagery, Blake employs mystical visions and biblical parables to explore both illumination and terror. Like all the poems in the book, "The Tyger" is written in the form of a childlike refrain, and depicts the complex interweaving of darkness and light in Creation. The wild cat is a predator, a fierce animal of terrifying beauty, smoldering and destructive, a Promethean figure of fire and death. Its unfathomable violence poses an enigma for the universe.

Tyger Tyger, burning bright,
In the forests of the night;
What immortal hand or eye,
Could frame thy fearful symmetry?
. . . .
When the stars threw down their spears
And water'd heaven with their tears
Did he smile his work to see
Did he who made the Lamb make thee?

Unlike the poem about the lamb, the tiger's innocent double, with its crystal clear responses, this poem is composed like a cascade of unanswered questions. I like the illustration, whose strange tiger, very different from the tiger you imagine as you read the poem, bears no resemblance to the real animal, seems neither threatening nor enraged, just an odd, slightly ungainly beast with a human head that nonetheless is the embodiment of evil on earth.

Did he who made the Lamb make thee? I am obsessed by this question. It is so close to the fundamental question that shuts off the process of rational analysis, marking the moment when you have no choice but to abandon it. And perhaps to resume thinking, but in a different form, a spiritual form that not everyone is prepared to explore. Am I and my rapist made from the same clay? To what extent do we resemble each other? Is there really a way for me to understand? These questions get confused, they don't all have the same meaning, nor do they all refer to the same processes, but they all burn with the same fire.

If we are all equal, created by the same energy, the tiger and the lamb will end up as one, according to the same

logic that led the Marquis de Sade to declare that good and evil come from the same indifferent life source. Of course to me the tiger is the rapist. So when I saw that she had chosen *Tiger, Tiger* as the title of a memoir about sexual violence, I silently congratulated Margaux. Well played, my friend, I thought.

Why? Why this? Why me? It's a familiar question in victims' accounts. It can be at the root of the desire to confront the aggressor, notably in the case of those who have subsequently disappeared from the victims' lives. Some people will seek out their abusers in order to ask them face to face. You can't help this need to understand, and yet therein lies the terrible frustration, for whether an abuser is an imbecile or endowed with a sadistic intelligence, in either case he is incapable of offering a response that sheds any light on why he did it. All he can do is talk about himself, his point of view, his conscious or unconscious motivations. Even if you were picked out from among other children, there's no explanation for why, no reason that might give you the key to moving on. For the choice is never because of something to do with you, it is always because of something to do with him. Many sexual predators have narcissistic personalities; they're capable of talking nonstop about themselves and, particularly if they were themselves once victims too, they may even succeed in drawing their victims into a kind of deluded compassion.

This inability to pinpoint the culprit in them, to understand the origin of their evil, to locate an imbalance that might be restored, also prevents us from fulfilling the need to make sense of what happened to us, and thus to bring about justice.

For his first book on the Rwandan genocide, Jean Hatzfeld began by gathering testimonies from the victims, aware they could not be expected to resolve the mystery of the hatred of which they had been the object. Three years later, while interviewing the murderers in prison for his second book, he realized that they too could not help us understand. *The mischief-makers [. . .] keep secrets in their souls*, says one of the prisoners, but nothing in what they tell Hatzfeld enables us to pierce those secrets. As Hannah Arendt showed us, genocidal murderers cannot allow themselves to think about what they have done, and it is this very absence of reflection that enables them to survive. Hatzfeld is stunned to discover that the men he interviews don't suffer from nightmares. *Is it possible? Of all war criminals, it is the genocidal killer who is the least tormented.* If they have regrets about their disastrous lives and cursed lot, they keep them to themselves. They all present themselves as decent guys who will one day, thanks to the victims' clemency, be given the freedom to get on with their lives, just like before the genocide.

Asked what leads soldiers to commit violent acts of rape in conflict zones, a well-known historian of the two world wars responded, *Because they can*. It sounds almost cavalier, but he said it in a tone of profound melancholy, the conclusion of a lifetime of research into conflict, violence, and depravity. They rape because they can, because society lets them, and when a man is allowed to rape, he will. It is as if the potential for evil is ever present in all of us; in conditions where brutality is possible, it will inevitably manifest. This is truly the theater of cruelty.

In 2017, six years after *Tiger, Tiger* was published, Margaux Fragoso was back in the newspapers. She'd died of ovarian cancer, at the age of thirty-eight. I've never been tempted to believe my hippie friends' arcane theories drawing a link between what had happened to me as a child and my cancer, but I was struck by the coincidence.

While I was lying in the Hôpital de la Conception in Marseille, a friend whom I'd lost touch with when I'd gone to live abroad was being treated for lung cancer in another hospital not far away called La Timone. We'd been close friends, years before, during the years I was living in Marseille. Four or five years older than me, he had moved to the city from faraway and, like me, been struck down by serious illness in the prime of life. As a child he was abused by his father's wife, like in a fairy tale, the wicked stepmother eaten up by jealousy. She treated him like a slave, locked him in the closet, humiliated him. He ran away when he was a teenager and lived a life on the margins of society that could be glorious at times but was often toxic, falling into periods of deep depression and taking out his anger on those weaker than himself, abandoning his children, beating his girlfriends, doing a whole host of appalling things, but never quite falling into absolute abjection, somehow always managing to cling on to the edge of the abyss, looking for a way out. He lived in a squat, a windowless garage, in the La Plaine neighborhood, worked for a cabinetmaker by day, and spent his nights striding through the city, or playing violent video games, or organizing full-scale role-playing tournaments with other lost souls who liked to pretend they were druids or medieval knights. He'd always dreamed of moving away, far from the city, with its hard drugs and temptations. Somehow, he eventually made it to Guyana, where he lived like Robinson Crusoe in a wooden cabin he built himself. The year of my cancer he was urgently repatriated to mainland France, with a stomach swollen like a balloon and lungs filled with liquid. A mutual friend told me that of our group of friends at the time, we were the two who'd had the most fucked-up childhoods.

Before committing to surgery, in desperation I went to see a mystical therapist recommended by some Mexican friends. She was a beautiful woman with a lustrous mane of long brown hair. Everything about her was gentle: her voice, her presence, her hands. She held my gaze and listened as I told her about my cyst. Before she began placing obsidian rocks on different parts of my body and asking me to imagine colored geometric forms linking my organs one to the other, she laid her hands on my swollen belly where the bulge of the tumor made me look as though I were three months pregnant. A cyst, she said, is an envelope containing mostly liquid. A pouch filled with tears.

She is not alone in thinking this. Scientists have for a while been working on the relationship between abuse and the subsequent development of certain illnesses whose conclusions, though obviously formulated as a different category of ideas and in a distinct scientific idiom, are not so different from those of my occult-minded friends.

Groundbreaking studies undertaken in the 1990s suggested a causal link not only with health problems resulting from toxic behaviors but also with other apparently unrelated symptoms. The commonsense conclusion would be that abuse leads to depression and the inability to look after oneself, explaining poor nutrition and risky behaviors like addiction that end up causing illnesses linked to unhealthy lifestyles. Yet many of the patients in these trials didn't fall into this category, they neither smoked nor drank, and didn't come from deprived backgrounds. The missing link came later, with the evolution in neuroscience showing how trauma can have an impact on hormone production, neural circuitry, the immune system, and even an individual's DNA.

Research on experiences of adversity in childhood (*adverse childhood experience*, or ACE) has been the catalyst for an entirely new way of considering the issue. Using a questionnaire to identify sources of difficulties experienced in childhood (for example violence, abandonment, or loss of a parent), it has been shown that it is possible to determine a link between an individual's physical and mental health later in life.

> *The higher the ACE score, the worse the outcome, on almost every measure, from addictive behavior to chronic disease, Paul Tough wrote in an article for The New Yorker. Compared with people who had no history of ACEs, those with ACE scores of 4 or higher were twice as likely to smoke, seven times as likely to be alcoholics, and six times as likely to have had sex before the age of fifteen. They were twice as likely to have been diagnosed*

with cancer, twice as likely to have heart disease, and four times as likely to suffer from emphysema or chronic bronchitis. Adults with an ACE score of 4 or higher were twelve times as likely to have attempted suicide than those with an ACE score of 0.

For those who suffered sexual abuse in childhood, the results are similar: Child victims grow into adults at risk of multiple disorders, from mental health problems, in particular bipolar disorder, to bodies haunted by all manner of dysfunction. It is slightly bizarre to think about it as a score, as if suffering can be quantified. *What's your score? I got 4. Not bad. I got 10 because my brother has Down syndrome. My mom committed suicide, what's that worth?* But numbers allow ideas to gain traction more decisively than intuition, as is often the way Western knowledge functions in the twenty-first century. Numbers talk. Twelve times more likely to have attempted suicide, forty-seven times more likely to have taken hard drugs. Which is a lot.

The year I had surgery for ovarian cancer, my friend Christian died of lung cancer a few streets away. I'd been planning to visit him when I got better. I thought we'd help each other and laugh at this unlikely coincidence. But it took me longer than I'd imagined to recover from what was not minor surgery. I never got to visit him. He was in his early forties.

He died and I'm alive. What do you do with a thought like that? When I told my teenage girlfriends my incest story, they must have wondered the same thing. All those years I was happily climbing trees while she was being raped. It could have been me, but it wasn't.

Coping

You often find in books by survivors the notion that they don't want to *adopt the attitude of a victim* or *be thought of as a victim*. What does that mean, exactly? Usually it's about refusing to be seen as an object of pity. But why should a victim be systematically viewed through the lens of pity, that strange combination of compassion and condescension?

I can't help thinking it's slightly absurd. It's not possible to have been raped yet not be a victim. A person who has been raped is a victim of rape, of an assault committed on her against her will.

In a documentary about the six girls and young women kidnapped by the Belgian rapist and serial killer Marc Dutroux, a journalist says of one of them, "Look at her, she rebuilt her life, she refuses to be a victim, she has a boyfriend, she has a sex life!" As if by having sex she expunges the rape, and by rebuilding her life she somehow ceases to be the girl who was once held prisoner by that monster. As if by coping, she has moved on and is no longer a victim. As if that were the objective, the only possible objective, to move on.

I loathe the idea that some people cope while others don't, and that getting over trauma is a morally laudable goal. I'm appalled by a hierarchy that makes the person who recovers, in contrast with the person who cannot, a superhuman being.

I used to think that too. I was proud of my resilience. It was thanks to my friend Edmond, the one who talked to a psychiatrist about me and persuaded me to go to the police, that I first discovered the concept. What does she do to cope? the psychiatrist asked him. She's studying, she reads a lot, all the time, maybe it's a symptom, an escape from real life. No, it's good, it's very good, this reader of Boris Cyrulnik decided, she'll get through this with books.

She will be *saved by literature*. I'm sure that's what he wanted to say, sitting there in his armchair, his back to the bookshelves, a Mozart symphony playing softly on the record player. I wanted to believe it, I wanted to believe that the kingdom of literature would welcome me like yet another orphan who found refuge there, but it turns out that even through art it is impossible to defeat despair. Literature did not save me. I am not saved.

I used to lump together all the things that made me who I am, the mountains where I was born, my parents and their working-class roots, the egalitarian French education system, with the rape just another thing in the baggage it was my lot to bear. I might as well have claimed as my own that beautifully wrought sentence from Jean-Paul Sartre's book on Jean Genet that the writer and philosopher Didier Eribon once designated the very principle of existence: *What matters is not what is done to us, but what we do with what is done to us.*

In order to be free, I was going to have to choose what baggage I wanted to hang on to and what I could lose. I wanted to believe that every human being, whatever their social class, race, sex, or culture, starts out in life with the same existential challenge: Free yourself of what you don't want, affirm what makes you thrive. I wanted to believe that I could deem the abuse I'd suffered to be just one element among many. And yet I had to acknowledge that there are fathomless differences between the possible categories of *what has been done to us*.

It takes courage and bravery to recover, to refuse to be destroyed. I like the passage in *King Kong Theory* where Virginie Despentes, quoting Camille Paglia, proposes that we consider rape from a different angle: Think of it as a risk worth taking. If you want to move around freely, you have to accept the possibility of bad luck. *If it happens to you, pick yourself up, dust yourself off, and move on.* Even though later on she had to recognize the enduring persistence of traumatic experience, I've always envied her initial reaction: *I figured I'd dealt with it, that I was thick-skinned, that I had better fucking things to do with my life than allow three loser dickwads to traumatize me.*

How I would love to be able to say that, and for it to be true. For ages I believed that my victory over him would be that I had coped, I hadn't let it defeat me, I hadn't given him that pleasure. But as it turned out, the fact that I moved on with my life was an element in his favor, letting him off the hook for what he'd done to me. There is no victory over him, and he doesn't care. He's been out of my life for years. And when you grew up being raped, it's a misapprehension to talk about getting over it.

Pick yourself up and move on doesn't apply when it comes to child abuse. Because for a child, this "you," who is simultaneously the object of the sentence, the "you" in the words *pick yourself up*, and the speaking subject of the narrative who says these words to encourage another person, a person who hears the injunction—everyone in this miniature world has been raped, and the rape is now, always and will be forever, a part of you. You cannot *pick yourself up* and free yourself of something that is literally a part of who you are. Your whole world is perceived through that filter. For a person who has known only that, everything is organized around this oppression. There is no unsubjugated self, no equilibrium to which one can return once the violence has ceased.

Shalamov writes that a stay in jail can be character forming, but torture leads to total collapse. Child sexual abuse is not an ordeal, an accident of life; it is a profound and systematic humiliation that destroys the very foundations of the self. If you have ever been a victim of it, you are always a victim. And you will be a victim forever. For even if you recover, you never truly recover.

Oh, all these pompous words. I'm getting carried away. I shouldn't generalize, there are so many ways to get things wrong; it's much safer to simply talk about my own experience. There are people who can actually imagine children taking pleasure from the act. The Italian writer Goliarda Sapienza's novel *The Art of Joy* opens in 1900 on the island of Sicily, where a little girl of five, the precociously sexual Modesta, persuades a teenage boy to perform cunnilingus on her. A few years later, aged nine, she loses her virginity to a stranger who claims to be her father; there is again pleasure in the sexual experience, until it turns into rape. Readers often interpret these episodes as evidence of the precocity of Modesta, with her immodest predilections, seeing her as an emblem of freedom with no limits. Sapienza is one of several authors I admire who write fiction about incest and childhood sexual awakening, in which girls and young women are not only at ease but even sometimes make the first move.

Then there are those who argue that imposing an age of consent implies that children and adolescents are stupid, without intelligence, sexual impulses, or free will. Guy Hocquenghem, Michel Foucault and Tony Duvert are notorious in France for having fought in the 1970s for pedophilia to be decriminalized, deploring the inclination for adults, usually women, to keep a constant eye on everything their children do, imprisoning them in a system of surveillance, inhibiting their development, blind to their true nature and the kingdom of desire. *After all*, Foucault once declared in an interview on the radio station France Culture, *an age limit fixed by law doesn't make much sense. Let me repeat, we can trust a child to say yes or no, he has or has not suffered violence.* It is easy enough to reject such an argument when it's made by someone with predatory inclinations. But when it's the child herself who is speaking, it's clearly more complicated. Spanish writer and performance artist Diana J. Torres writes about having had more than sixty lovers by the age of sixteen, some of whom paid for her services, including one man who took her out on his sailboat and talked to her about Pasolini and his marital problems:

> *I had all the power in that relationship, Alain was just a puppet who let me hold the strings, he completely acquiesced to*

the perverted desires of a little girl; but because of this deplor-
able attitude that maintains that kids who are underage are
idiots, no judge would have seen this case through such a lens.
[. . .] If I'd wanted to, I could have ruined his whole life with
a single phone call accusing him of child abuse, or I could have
blackmailed him and made a packet.

I can just about conceive of a little girl desiring an adult at the level of fantasy as she experiences her own sexual awakening, but the idea that she might take any real satisfaction from the act or that she would choose to do it again seems genuinely unlikely. But what is true for me isn't necessarily true for someone else. This image of the abused child controlling her destiny is seductive precisely because it's transgressive, it allows us to conceive of a victim who doesn't conform to society's injunction that she be destroyed by what she has suffered. In a way I wish I could be like that, not only because I'd like to be cool, and transgression is always cooler than obedience, but also because it suggests a means of restoring the complexity of contradictory perceptions. I wish I had Torres's brute strength, her freedom, her revolutionary fervor. I haven't succeeded in liberating myself by the Promethean creation of dissident sexualities, but I've always been drawn to their unruly boldness. Why not listen to the voices that contradict everything we think we know about child victims?

Well, for one thing, this lauding of ironclad resilience, this valorization of the superhuman beings who do recover, seems to me to lean toward a dangerous glorification that condemns those who know they won't recover to even greater despair. On the other hand, I worry that by focusing on the shattering aftermath I tend toward puritanism, endorsing the received belief that a child who has been raped is doomed, their life ruined.

Were there any moments of joy? Of course. Not, for me, in the act itself. I've dug deep into my memories but can find no trace at all. But this doesn't mean that my entire childhood was shrouded in gloom. A young person will always find some crack in the space to be happy. You know deep down you have only one childhood, one adolescence, and if you can't find a taste for ordinary life there's no point in sticking around. I had fields of tall grasses to hide in while the other children, squealing with laughter, shouted my name, mountain streams with icy water tumbling over gray stones, summer storms, swollen raindrops on my cheeks, cherry trees to clamber up and pick the fruit. I had a blonde-haired sister who was not much younger than me, and we got to look after two more little ones, a curly-headed brother and a skinny, giggly sister, whom we adored. During the summer vacation, when our parents traveled long distances to work, we were left alone for days on end under the vague surveillance of an aunt or a grandmother. Left to our own devices. Free. I can say I was happy, we were happy. No one can take away the summer rain from us.

Juxtapositions

I keep coming back to the question of torture. A parallel I can't help drawing though I don't like it. In my mind's eye, almost unconsciously, everywhere I look I see what happened to me. I'll be reading something and out of the blue a word or a sentence will trigger a kind of electric shock and take me back to the mechanics of the rape. I was leafing through a doctoral thesis about punishment under Pinochet's regime for an essay I was writing about contemporary Chilean literature, in which the writer analyzes the psychological consequences of torture and explains that it creates a borderline, a rupture with reality. *During torture, everything rational is absurd.* I found it hard not to appropriate this statement to describe my own experience. It applies perfectly to the systematic rape of a child, which imposes a logical adaptation, i.e., survival, onto a system where logic is absent. It reminds me of all the pet phrases my stepfather used to come out with (You don't love me, so I rape you; you're a good girl, so I rape you; you've been naughty, you've annoyed me, so I rape you as a punishment; I love you, so I rape you). Does this mean it's possible to compare incest to torture? It's an extrapolation, I really should avoid the juxtaposition, but I can't help myself.

I know how shocking and unjustifiable people might find these comparisons. I shouldn't make them. I have this tendency to be overhasty when it comes to linking cause and consequence or making analogies. In this sense, my thought lacks rigor. I get carried away, confused, my mind runs amok. But it's hardly surprising, especially when one considers the lack of philosophical writing on the subject. Thought fuels its own fire. Thought, as Deleuze would have it, uses the whole world to feed its fire.

I've never read any feminist theory. I'm sure I'd find answers there. I don't know why I haven't looked. I didn't come across it when I was younger. Maybe I didn't want to read books that put words to my experience. I don't know. Any answers I have found have been drawn from outside the field of incest and rape inquiry, indeed from outside the field of critical thinking in general. I have constructed myself through fiction, which offers only oblique, tangential responses based on stories that aren't real.

I learned to think about violence from novels about slavery, the Shoah, the Algerian War. Occasionally I make equivalences that need to be adjusted or qualified because however traumatic it is, sexual abuse cannot be compared in any way to crimes against humanity. Such misapprehensions can be explained by the peculiar circumstances of my intellectual formation.

There was no one I could talk to about what was happening to me. As I grew older, I gradually began to realize that I had been reduced to a position of servitude, of absolute subjugation. I started to wonder about the meaning of it all. There were episodes of incest in the novels I borrowed from the libraries at school and in the village, but it was treated simplistically, as a dreadful yet banal tragedy that the character could do nothing about, that condemned women to brief, tragic, suicidal lives. In Zola, for example, the favorite of literature teachers when I was in junior high and still, I fear, today, rape is a tragedy common to women and children that leads inexorably to a life of exploitation, prostitution, depression, and early and violent death.

At high school at the end of the 1980s, we were immersed in the study of the Second World War in history class, deluged with texts each more interesting than the last about the concentration camps, the memory of the persecuted, the inconceivable crime of genocide. The question of language and art were central. Is it possible to write after Auschwitz? And if so, what? Is the infinite circle of revenge the only possible outcome of oppression? This desolate landscape became the imaginary terrain onto which I projected my own need to comprehend what I was going through. How to think the unthinkable. Tell the untellable. Face the limits of the human.

Aleksandr Solzhenitsyn. Primo Levi. Imre Kertész. André Brink. Toni Morrison. Their writings about the concentration camp universe, apartheid, and slavery offered me ways to think about radical evil, to consider the guilt of the survivor, to touch the threshold of resilience.

In the same way, my own experience of extreme subjugation is what makes it possible for me to grapple with thinking about other types of trauma.

After she'd finished her degree in anthropology, my childhood friend Marianne, the first person I ever talked to about the rape, went back to live on the outskirts of Briançon. She's a documentary filmmaker. Around ten years ago the first refugees began to arrive in the region where we grew up, crossing Alpine passes on foot after security measures were reinforced at the Italian border further south. Marianne made a film about some of their intertwined journeys. She shared with me something she'd read that had moved her deeply, about the psychological wounds of people who'd been held in Syrian jails. The fact that they arrived at the end of their journey traumatized and shattered cannot be solely attributed to the multiple challenges of reaching Europe. They had seen evil in the eyes of their torturers, had been confronted by the impossibility of denying the human capacity for cruelty. Now they can never escape it. Even those who manage to get residency papers, even those who reached the goal they had set themselves when they left their homeland, remain forever imprisoned by what they have seen.

I recognize in this something of what I am tentatively feeling my way to expressing about my own life: how having been forced to spend time on the dark side means my own innocence can never be restored.

Of course, I'm not suggesting that my ordeal can be compared with that of a victim of torture any more than I can compare the basement of my childhood to a barracks in Auschwitz. But concepts of violence can be transferred from one field to another.

It's similar, in a way, to the risk inherent in writing a book in which I can't really go beyond a personal investigation and the telling of my own story: I'm exposing myself to the possibility that readers will tease out certain details and use them out of context. My words will be misinterpreted, warped, twisted to mean different things. That's the way thought reproduces itself, not by spreading across a network of rhizomes or roots but by random pollination.

I long believed I was the only prisoner in the cellar, despite a rational intuition that this feeling must be an illusion born of trauma and societal taboo. I suspected there were other children suffering similar experiences. I never dared ask any of my rebellious adolescent friends, but it seemed to me that among those who had nothing to lose, who destroyed any chance of being safe, who ran away from home, who slept around, there must have been kids who had gone through something similar, not necessarily the same kind of abuse, but something like it.

We would all of us have been less alone if I had spoken out. What stopped me? The thing is, if you don't talk about something, it doesn't exist. I suppose I preferred not to bring it into existence, to leave it in the shadows.

When I began telling people, after I left home at the age of seventeen, I was startled: Every time I'd talk about it with someone I'd be told about a rape that was suffered either by the person I was talking to, or their close friend or relative. Every single time. I began to assume the hidden fact of this systematic violence lay pretty much everywhere. It was this instinct that led me to agree to a public trial rather than a closed hearing, often the victim's preference in such cases. It seemed like the right decision, and I also thought it would free me from the obligation to write about it one day.

What was it that made me change my mind? Perhaps the simple fact that I made it out the other side. I am no longer the vulnerable little girl that I once was. Now it's my turn to be the protector.

How I talked about it to my daughter

Places are a way of dating moments in her childhood as well. I remember a conversation on a beach in Cancún. I know the exact age she was because I know when that holiday took place, it's part of our family lore. Max was taking part in a conference, and she and I went sightseeing every day while we waited for it to be over so we could leave for Mérida, where we were going to stay with friends. The conversation took place on the beach one day, in the wake of an earlier conversation we'd had at home.

I'd been steeling myself in preparation for a while. Talking can be part of a prevention strategy, depending on how far you're willing to go, and it has to be a dialogue with the child. You can't just tell a child to say no, their body belongs to them and no one else has the right to touch it. That's what most programs aimed at preventing sexual abuse do, but it's like teaching consent to someone who doesn't have the means to consent or otherwise. A child can't say no to their big brother or teacher, such a no would be unthinkable for them. And then if something does happen to them, you can't expect them to tell you if you haven't already brought it up, prepared them, welcomed the conversation. You need ideas to imagine things, words to say them, context to receive them.

I was worried about doing my job as a parent, and telling her about my life. I knew the moment would come when I was going to have to tell her. It ended up being much more natural than I'd dared hope. I'd mentioned in her presence several times that my childhood hadn't been easy. I used the term abuse. One day she asked me out of the blue (though it's never really out of the blue but, like the iceberg, we can only ever see the tip) what exactly he did to me.

—Did your papa beat you?

—No, that's not what he did, he didn't beat me.

—Oh. Right. So what did he do?

—Do you know what sexual abuse is?

—No.

—It's when a grown-up makes you do sexual things with them.

—What's that?

—Well . . . he touched my private parts. He wanted me to touch his. He made me put his penis in my mouth.

—*Wacala!* (The Mexican expression came spontaneously to her as an expression of disgust, it's stronger than, say, gross, it's what you say when you want to express really deep revulsion.)

I took the opportunity to ask her if anyone had ever tried to do something like that to her or any of her friends. I told her I was always there for her if anything happened, and that if she was victim or witness to something like that, she mustn't try to deal with it on her own, she must talk to an adult she trusted, it could be me or someone else. Yes, she said, in that way she has when she isn't really listening.

And that was it, she didn't ask anything more, nothing to do with that anyway, she changed the subject, and I knew we'd have to carry on the conversation another time, it had been too brief, she obviously hadn't understood. But as it turned out, she'd understood very well.

It was a few weeks, maybe a month or two later, that we traveled down to the Yucatán Peninsula. We were staying with friends; a couple, both students, who lived in a half-constructed new neighborhood on the outskirts of Puerto Morelos. The little house was a cement cube surrounded by a square of bare earth that would one day be a garden. It was unbearably hot. The young woman went off every morning with Max to attend roundtable discussions on rural tourism, while her boyfriend shut himself inside the only room with air-conditioning to try and work on his dissertation. My daughter and I went out to explore, spending the day in whatever cool spot we could find. We went to the town square, or we took the bus to the beach to spend the afternoon.

One day we went to Cancún. I remember looking on the internet for a public beach between the hotels. I found a beautiful spot. The sky was overcast. We built castles on the soft, white sand. In the middle of digging a tunnel she began asking me the questions that she should have asked (or so I thought) the first time.

—That thing he did to you, your papa.

—He wasn't exactly my papa.

—Whatever, that thing he did to you, why didn't you tell your mom?

I paused for a moment. She carried on patting damp sand onto a tower, waiting for me to speak.

—I couldn't. When something like that happens, you can't tell your mom if she doesn't ask. It's very odd. It's like the words get stuck in your throat, they can't get out. I think I was scared.

—You were scared he'd kill you?

—Yes.

We kept on building the sandcastle. I wasn't focused at all, but it didn't matter, we had the whole afternoon. This time she didn't stop at one question. She asked them all.

—What about Rose, did he do it to her too? And your other sister? Is it something that happens to brothers too? Why didn't you tell your grandma or your teacher? Did you cry? At school, or just at home? Didn't anyone ask you why you were crying? Why did you lie?

I know now that there are worse things than what happened to me. I don't even have to look too far: What happened to my mother is maybe one of the worst things that can happen. Worse than anything you can imagine. The rape and torture, for years, of the little girl you brought into the world.

Some people say that when you become a parent you relive your own childhood, as if giving yourself a new chance to enter that land. We're told not to project too much onto our children. It would make them suffer. It would deprive them of their freedom to be themselves. *Your children are not your children*, and all that. But when you've been a child who was raped, it's impossible not to project when you have your own children, or when people you love have theirs. I'd go so far as to say that it's practically impossible not to be projecting all the time onto every child you ever meet. It takes intense mental effort to function normally in the company of children who are with the adults who are supposed to take care of them.

You're sitting with a girlfriend on a park bench. You've been for a walk and now you're having a cigarette, still chatting. The play area is full of children. Sandbox, slides, swings, shady areas not too far from the benches where mothers keep a watchful eye on their kids. They don't look at them constantly, but they see them. All the children are with someone, being watched, some more attentively than others, by parents and babysitters. There are a few fathers there. Without breaking off or changing the subject, it occurs to you to wonder if the fathers are going to rape their children when they get back from the park. Or if on the way home in the car for lunch that the mother is preparing, they're going to stop by the side of the road just long enough for a little blow job, or wait till tonight in the bath, or at bedtime, before a goodnight hug. It flashes through your mind. You don't say anything to your friend, though you briefly lose the thread of the conversation, but you pick it up and carry on chatting. You're barely aware of having thought it.

You're at a birthday party. There's a little one who needs to pee, he looks round to see who can take him to the bathroom. A teenage cousin says he'll go with him, he takes him by the hand and off they go together. You follow them with your eyes, regretting that you weren't quicker to respond.

You walk past a lesson at the tennis club. The trainer is massaging the ankles of a teenage girl.

A friend tells you that her daughters, aged seven and twelve, are going on a weeklong spiritual retreat camp with their catechism group.

You're on the bus. A little girl is asleep, lying with her head in a man's lap.

I can't stop myself spying. I used to do it when I was a kid, to make sure the others were safe. I'm always spying even now, sometimes absentmindedly, sometimes with intent. I spy on the fathers in the changing room at the pool, the teachers who see students in their office. I spy on people I meet in the street, my friends, my neighbors. I spy on my partner. He knows that I love him, that I trust him. I think he knows that I spy on him, and that I can't not. I think he forgives me.

While I'm writing these pages, Céline Sciamma's movie, *Petite Maman*, comes out in theaters. It's about a little girl, suffering after her grandmother has died and her mother is absent, lost in her grief, who meets a girl her own age in the woods, or perhaps she imagines her, her mother when she was a child. It's such a beautiful idea. My daughter often asks me to tell her about when I was little. I don't know if she's trying to imagine herself in my place. I wish I could get to know her from the perspective of a child instead of always being the adult who organizes her life. To become her friend. How wonderful that would be.

My thoughts begin to wander. I try to picture myself as a little girl inside her life, the sheltered life I never knew. Would I have turned into the same me when I grew up? If not, who would I have become? What about me inside Max's life, loved and cherished by two normal parents, or inside the lives of my friends who grew up with single mothers or in children's homes? Would I still be me? Have I gained anything by experiencing what I did? Or lost something? If I've gained, or learned something, how can I pass it on to her, without her experiencing it? If I've lost something, what must I do to ensure she does not inherit my wounds?

My daughter is ten. She's always loved hugs and massages. Sometimes at bedtime she asks me to run my hands through her hair or stroke her back. She likes to fall asleep like that.

My hand moves over her smooth back. She is still tanned from the summer. She is skinny, like I was. I can feel her vertebrae sticking out like hard little hummocks beneath her skin. I move slowly up and down her back the way she likes it. I'm alone with her in the bedroom and I begin to envision what I could do to her. All it would take is for my hand to change direction and slip down into her panties. I could stroke her little slit if I wanted to. She'd be so surprised she wouldn't dare say anything. I could put my finger inside her, it's just a matter of a few centimeters, and our lives would be changed forever.

My hand stops. I want to turn on the light, to leave the room.

Maman, don't stop.

I start rubbing her back again. I slow my breathing. Just out of curiosity, to see what happens when you do something like that. Are there people who do it just because they can, to shatter the mirror, to see what happens if they stop obeying the rules? I'm almost sure she wouldn't say anything. And if she did, it would be easy enough to manipulate her so she wouldn't put up a fight. I could sweet-talk her, make her think it's just a cuddle, or bribe her like I do when I want her to tidy her room. The classic Saturday morning cartoon bribe. If you don't do what I'm asking, no TV. Or I could threaten her. Tell her how awfully sad I'd be if she were to tell anyone. The family would be broken up. I might even go to jail. Is that what you want?

Maman, why do you keep stopping? If you don't do it properly, I'm never going to fall asleep.

I concentrate, try to do it right so she falls asleep, so

I can escape from this bubble of softness and shadow. Toying with these thoughts is a way of torturing myself a bit. I know I could never hurt her. But I can sense the border between good and evil. I can guess what they feel, the rush of crazed energy, the adrenaline. The sexual thrill. It could happen.

Maman, I'm not sleepy anymore. Will you tell me a story?

Once upon a time there was a very kind King who had eight children, seven boys and a girl. The King was a widower. He adored his children and brought them up with lots of love but one day he was put under a spell that made him fall in love. He married again, a woman who was cunning and mean and who took against the seven princes. She had magic powers. She cast an evil spell over the brothers that turned them into swans, and kept behind only the little girl to be her servant. The brothers flew off to live in a faraway kingdom and the little girl had no idea what had happened to them.

The father was very fond of his new wife and the princess didn't dare tell him how horribly she treated her. She missed her beloved brothers and wept much of the time.

Years went by before she saw them again. One day she was walking alone in the woods near the castle when she heard the rustling of wings over by the lake. As she began walking toward it, she saw seven magnificent swans perched at the water's edge. The sun was beginning to set and, as she watched, the swans changed into princes. She ran toward them. But the joy of their reunion was short-lived: They could only maintain their human form for one hour. The brothers told their sister of their misfortune and explained the reason for their exile: They could only return to their childhood home once a year. To get there they had to cross an ocean out of which rose, when the tide was at its lowest, a small island, which only happened one day a year. They stopped on the island at sunset to spend an hour in human form, before turning back into swans.

—Take me with you, begged the girl. I'll make myself useful. I can't be apart from you any longer!

The brothers talked among themselves, and agreed that they would try to take their sister with them, each in turn carrying her on his back. They left the following day.

The journey took longer than usual because the weight of the princess slowed their flight. The sun was getting lower, and the island still had not appeared on the horizon. The helpless princess clung to the neck of her eldest brother, wondering if they were all about to die because of her. And then, at the very last moment, a little rock rose up in the middle of the sea. It was the island. They spent an hour there, huddling together, and as soon as the brothers had turned back into swans, continued on their journey. The following day they reached a beautiful country, where the brothers led a peaceful life in a forest, and there was no risk of anyone ever witnessing their metamorphosis.

And so began the young woman's strange but happy life with her brothers. At night she slept in a grotto on a bed of branches, while her days were spent in complete solitude, waiting impatiently for the return of her brothers at dusk. One day a fairy appeared to her in the grotto and told her there was a way to reverse the spell.

—You must gather nettles and use them to weave shirts for your brothers. Once you have finished, you must fling the shirts, all at the same time, onto your brothers' backs at the very moment of their metamorphosis. If you dare to try, know that you may not utter another word from this moment on, or the magic will be broken.

The young woman agreed. Over the days that followed she gathered nettles and then began to weave. At first the brothers wanted to know what she was doing, but they soon figured it out. Grateful for her efforts, they helped her as much as they could, bringing masses of nettles in their beaks for her work.

One day a prince from a neighboring kingdom was riding through the forest. The moment he saw her he fell in love with the silent young woman weaving shirts by the lake. He gathered her up and carried her off to his kingdom. She managed to hide the finished shirts beneath her dress and to bring a bundle of nettles with her. The prince installed her in a beautiful bedchamber whose windows looked out over magnificent gardens. He could not understand why she carried on with her weaving. But he was deeply in love and when he saw that she wept when her work was taken away from her, he let her carry on. People whispered behind his back. It was said that he was bewitched. The king's counselors were convened, and they declared that the young woman would be burned at the stake if she refused to explain herself to the people.

The princess had no choice but to continue her task. She was running out of nettles, and the day of the trial was approaching. She wove and wove, in silence, day and night, up to the very last moment. The day of the sentencing arrived. She ascended the tribune, unable to say a word to defend herself. She simply carried on weaving the final shirt, clutching the others to her breast beneath her robes.

The verdict was passed. The pyre was ready. The prince, mad with grief, wept and begged for mercy. He was granted just a few hours, until the sun set, to sit with his wife in her cell. He begged her to speak, but she kept silent. Guards arrived to take her to the square where she was to be burned to death. At the very moment they reached there, seven majestic swans swooped down and positioned themselves at the young woman's feet. She leapt up from her jailors to embrace them, and just as the light of the setting sun began to glow, flung the shirts over the swans. The brothers immediately regained their human shape. At last the young woman could speak, her brothers explained everything, and she was saved.

All eight stayed in the kingdom and lived there together to the end of their days, the brothers at last released from the evil spell and the princess having regained her speech and her gladness. A single memory lingered of their strange adventure: The youngest of the brothers had only one arm, the other having kept the form of a swan's wing, because the young woman had not had time to complete his shirt and this part of his body had not been transformed.

In French, unlike in English, there is a literary tense, called the *passé simple*, or the simple past, always written and never spoken, that draws the reader into a parallel world that both exists and does not exist. In children's stories, characters barely out of childhood fly over oceans on the backs of magical creatures, climb mountains of salt, hide from ogres. There are manifold dangers, constant ill-treatment. To escape her father's lust, Peau d'âne, or Donkeyskin, hides her beauty by draping herself in a grotesque animal hide. Only its ugliness and pestilential odor protect her. She makes herself vile to escape her father's vileness. There is Cinderella, her sisters' scapegoat. The women killed by Bluebeard. Pinocchio, a victim of kidnapping and child trafficking. Hansel and Gretel, treated like slaves by a witch who fattens them up to eat them. Harry Potter, ill-treated by his uncle, his aunt and his cousin, forced to sleep in the closet under the stairs. All these little heroes and heroines valiantly overcoming all the adversity that life puts in their way (adverse childhood experience, to hark back to the more serious term), transposed into the world of fantasy, giving their readers advice on resilience, comforting us by making us believe that eventually luck does change. One day, a prince realizes there is a queen beneath that stinking cape, you find out you have magic powers, your nobility is revealed after a series of trials. One day, when you are older, intones the narrator, after bravely persisting for so long in the face of ill fortune, luck will smile upon you.

While we're talking fairy tales, let me tell you the legend of the rabbit on the moon.

One day Quetzalcoatl, the greatest and most powerful of the gods, went off on a journey around the world, garbed in human form. Because he had been walking all day, by the time night came he was seized by exhaustion and hunger. But he carried on walking until the stars began to glimmer and the moon appeared in the sky. He sat down to rest by the side of the road. That was when he spied a little rabbit that had emerged from its burrow.

—What are you eating? he asked the rabbit.

—Grass, replied the rabbit. Would you like some?

—No thank you, I don't eat grass.

—What are you going to do then?

—I'm going to die of hunger and thirst.

The rabbit hopped toward Quetzalcoatl and said,

—Listen, I'm just a little rabbit, but if you're hungry, you're welcome to eat me.

The god stroked the rabbit, and replied:

—That's very kind of you.

He continued to stroke the rabbit's soft, docile little head.

—From now on, the whole world will remember you. I want to honor your kindness and generosity.

And he picked up the rabbit and raised it above him, as high as he could, as high as the moon, where the rabbit's silhouette remains evermore.

Then the god came back down to earth and said to the rabbit,

—Your portrait will remain imprinted on the moon forever. You will always be a little rabbit but now the whole world will remember you.

Do you see the connection? Maybe there isn't really one, but what I see is yet another weak, vulnerable creature lauded for his self-sacrifice. We still eat rabbits, though that bit has been left out of the story. The god does not honor him for his altruism, but for the gift of his flesh.

Offering oneself in sacrifice to the most powerful, hiding from monsters, fathers and ogres, keeping silent—these are the lessons fairy tales teach us. The little rabbit will be rewarded, if not in this world, then in the next, he will remain in the memory of everyone who sees the glow of the moon in the middle of the night.

Because you don't have the choice when there is such an imbalance of power. You must hide in the shadows, flee if you can. One day the moment arrives for your escape. You flee to safety. But it feels strange to feel safe, because you know that the darkness does not cease to exist when you emerge from it. It reminds me of what Reinaldo Arenas says about exile: You escape from a burning house, you're safe, you find yourself in a welcoming land. But your house is still in flames.

Shame

You have looked evil in the eye and now no one can look at you. It is the legend of Medusa. After the rape no one can look her in the eye. Those who do are turned to stone. Her hatred is so intense it makes snakes grow out of her head instead of hair.

People stopped greeting me in the village. That's what happens in the countryside when you are ostracized: People stop talking to you, or even acknowledging you. You hear it all the time: So and so, I don't know what's up with him, he doesn't even say hallo to me anymore.

My mother was upset that the neighbors still greeted him after he'd come out of prison. She asked Mimi why she still spoke to him. Mimi was one of the old ladies I loved the most when I was a child. She had grown up in poverty in the upper part of the village. We used to go to her house and drink grenadine in the kitchen that smelled of hay and dung. Flies stuck to the waxed cotton tablecloth and we'd chase them with a finger as we listened to tales of her past. She loved me back, this old peasant woman who had never had children of her own. She used to tell me what a dream it would have been to study instead of tending sheep. She cried when I left for university.

My mother: I heard you and your brother are still talking to him.

Mimi: But he didn't do anything to us.

We know that what he did, he did to everyone. He did it to the whole village. Yet at the same time, they're not wrong, the villagers, all those people who pretended not to recognize me when I came back to the valley. It was I who had sullied the village's reputation. The disgrace was ours, but it was also theirs.

For years the village was known as the place where the rapist lived. Obviously it wasn't the only village where a rapist lived. But words forge a reputation. It is the denunciation that brings about the shame.

You must be prepared to lose a great deal when you decide to speak out. You're going to lose your family, obviously, but you're also going to lose your village, your childhood memories and illusions. What do you get in return? I don't know. The truth, I suppose, but what truth really is, I couldn't tell you.

Leave or stay

Is it necessary to leave in order to reinvent yourself? I left. To start with, I went somewhere a few hours away, then further, then further and further still. But it is never far enough away. I live in Mexico now. My sister Rose lives in Chile. Distant lands that we love in contradictory ways, and where we will never be entirely at home.

My other sister and brother stayed. What do they see when they look at the house where their father raped me? The house was sold, but they inherited the garage next door, which they renovated and turned into a small apartment. My youngest sister used to live there. She had a little table and chairs in her little patch of garden. On the other side of the hedge, the house she grew up in, the house we all grew up in. What did she see? Was she able to bring new life into this place, did she manage to paint colors over the black of death that still scars the landscape I see? Or did she resign herself to living with that death, seeing it there every morning on the other side of the hedge?

When you arrive in an unfamiliar place you only see what is visible. But in a place you know, you see both the visible and the invisible. What is no longer there, the stories you've been told, the legends and lives associated with every nook and cranny of the place.

The Basque writer Bernardo Atxaga writes about a stranger who moves to a village and becomes friends with the locals. One day, sitting on a low wall high on a hill overlooking a plateau, the stranger is chatting with two elderly men from the village about the particular nature of what they see down below on the plain that stretches before their eyes. One of the old men turns to the stranger and declares, *You may be cleverer than a rabbit, but I'll bet anything you like that you can't see as many things from here as I can.* The stranger tells him he is sure that he is right, and asks him to explain.

Because you only see what's there, whereas I see both what is there and what isn't there. He points to a path that crosses the plain below and vanishes into the distance. He knows where the path goes, and whenever he sees it, he thinks of the village it leads to, and pictures the village, with its fountain and its old houses. He goes further, explaining the difference between what a person sees who has spent their whole life in the same place, compared with what a person sees who comes from elsewhere. A villager like him sees the past in every place, every ruin, every tree he walks by.

> *When I see those trees, I see all the parties we held when we were young. I see the girls and the boys, I see Benito and myself. Not old and decrepit like we are now, but with our white shirts on and with all the grace of our twenty years. Isn't that marvelous?*

Do you think that's marvelous? It depends. It depends what kind of invisible things can be glimpsed through the visible.

When I sit and drink a cup of tea at the little table in my little sister's little garden, I see on the other side of the hedge the house where I grew up. I see the improvements made by the new owners, I see how the trees we planted when I was a child have grown. I see the other things as well. The basement where we lived for a year while the rest of the house was being renovated, for example. All of us sleeping in the same room. My mother who left at six in the morning to clean the offices in the Écrins National Park. I'm pretending to be asleep, but I need to get up to pee. I hold it in as long as I can. I know he's awake, I can hear him breathing behind the shelving that separate our beds from our parents' bed. I have to get up. We had a special pot to pee in. He hears me, calls my name, I climb into the bed. I try to remember what my sister did (not my youngest sister, who wasn't born yet, my other sister, two years younger than me). Did she hold it in as long as me? Did she end up getting into the bed too? Even after the move upstairs, we still spent a lot of time in the basement where the tools were stored. He'd take me out to work in the garden and we'd go down to the basement between two wheelbarrows of soil. I can still picture the old stone vaulting, beautifully restored, the grouting I scraped to get rid of the moss that had been growing there forever. I see the front of the house and behind it I see each room, before the renovation and after the renovation, I see each room and I see myself and I see him.

What does my sister see? Is her invisible so different from mine that she can stand seeing it every day? Does she see happy memories? Innocence? Or does she just see a house, a big, solid house in the Alps that once was a ruin and twenty years later has been beautifully restored?

It seems impossible to me that she doesn't see a haunted house. And what about the people who bought it? They got a bargain after the trial when the house was sold at a knockdown price. They couldn't not have known, they had family in the village. Everyone knew. They bought a house in whose rooms a little girl had been raped. In every single room. How could this house not be haunted? Even if you don't believe in ghosts, what do you have to do to not think about it? Opposite the house, in a little cottage, lives the sister of the little girl. They see her every day. Does it occur to them to wonder how she feels when they bump into her outside the house where she grew up and which she had to move out of when her father was sent to jail? Are they still pleased with themselves for having got such a bargain when they bought this lovely stone house in the mountains?

When I realized that to protect them, I would have to remain silent, I said nothing. At night I wandered around cemeteries. I wove shirts made out of nettles. When I thought that to protect them, I had to speak, I spoke. People told me I'd lose everything, I'd be called a witch and a traitor. I spoke anyway. I think that everything I did, I did to save them. To save them from what, exactly? For a long time I believed that they'd been spared the worst.

I'm not sure anymore.

Now they're adults, each struggling with their own demons, burdened by the one arm that never regained its human form. They do their best to hide it, but a swan's wing attached at the shoulder can't so easily be concealed.

One day, while we were drinking tea in her little garden, my sister told me that her father's greatest regret was having been absent during her adolescence, that she'd had to grow up without a father, worse still, with a father in jail. But I had to, I said, he might have raped you. She's sure he wouldn't have. He would never have done that. That's what he says, and she believes him. Why? Because they were his children, they were his flesh and blood, he'd never have laid a finger on them.

Soon after this conversation I go home, back to my country, my new country, still thinking about what my sister had said to me in her garden, about the visible and the invisible. I brood obsessively on her words. I share my despair with my friends. They tell me not to blame my sister, she is guilty of nothing, she is also just trying to get on with her life. Oh, come on, I say, if it had happened to her, she'd never have been able to forgive him. The only reason she can forgive him is because the victim was me not her. In order to keep on living she's doing the same thing as him, as all the others, denying what happened to me, not denying the facts, she can't, but she won't acknowledge how terrible it was. If I want to keep on loving my sister, I have to accept that she's forgiven him, that she thinks what he did is excusable, I have to forget, or at least pretend to, I have to act as though it wasn't me, as though it wasn't that bad, as though it had never happened. I suppose that's what I should have done from the beginning, then we wouldn't have had to suffer all these years for nothing.

Making a fresh start

After he comes out of prison, he sets off to walk the Camino de Santiago. In common with many prisoners, he had a spiritual awakening while he was behind bars. During the pilgrimage he meets a woman twenty years his junior, in other words almost the same age as I am, but she's an adult of course, because now he's forty-five. They fall in love. She is also deeply religious. It's perhaps her irrational side, her mystical fervor, that enables her to forgive him when she finds out what he did. She accepts him with her entire being, exactly as God sent him to her, with his sinful soul and his quest for redemption.

I'm fabricating here, but I have to. Frankly I can't understand how anyone could forgive, or even want to, how anyone would choose to be with someone who had raped a child, even if it was ten or twenty years ago, but I'll pass over that because this isn't about me or you but a young woman who, out of the goodness of her heart and her love for this man, manages to forgive all those who have offended her and overcome the obstacles the Lord has put in her way, so that she can prove her faith in Him and in life.

Hold on. Not only does she forgive him, she moves in with this man, sets up an organic farm, and has four children with him. Four! With us four that makes eight, the magic number of his dreams. They've bought a small stone building on a plot of land surrounded by forest, where they grow organic vegetables, and produce jams and preserves.

Plot twist: The farm is open to the public, they welcome groups of students and schoolchildren. They have the right to homeschool their children. The law can't stop them (before prison you are deemed innocent, and when you come out of prison you have served your sentence and so, like a deal with the Holy Spirit, you are newly innocent again). The only thing that could stop them would be proof that there had been a repeat offense—not a risk of a repeat offence, but an actual recurrence, in other words someone would have to slip into the house, hide in a room where he's alone with one of the children, and catch him in the act. Video evidence would be even better. A drone disguised as a fly maybe. But until that happens, the assumption is that there has been no repeat offense. You either believe that or you can't sleep at night.

I waver between the assumption that everything is for the best in the best of all possible worlds, or a world approaching it that doesn't include my rapist doing the same thing to another child, and the possibility that the nightmare is being repeated, day after day, night after night, with the slight variations peculiar to nightmares, which repeat but are never quite the same—for fear, like desire, is nourished by imagination.

Perhaps he won't start again. His life is back on track. He's found a wife who looks like a younger version of my mother (twenty years younger, the age I am now, but everybody does it, it's not meant to be a sign of control, love is ageless), she's unassuming, devoted to her family, her children's education, the organic farm. They've bought a ruined building in the countryside with a decent-sized plot of land. I picture them living in the house while it's being fixed up, all sleeping in the same room (they don't have the means to both rent an apartment and pay the mortgage, so they've moved into the construction site and one day each child will have their own room, right now it's still exciting, living in their own home, and doing it up themselves, it's the exact same story, almost the same except it's not as cold, they're not in the Alps, they have olive trees and it rarely snows). They make their own bread and jams and preserves. I bet they've planted quince trees, his favorite. He loves the fruit's distinctive scent, it takes him back to his childhood. They make quince jelly, it's never quite right, not like his mother made it. Start over, poach the quince, add sugar, mix, filter, spill it, it's so sticky, quince jelly, it gets onto every kitchen surface, wipe it all clean after each batch, shoo the flies away, start again, start again. But maybe he hasn't started again. Maybe he has gone right back to the beginning. Once upon a time there was a family who lived in the woods, cut off from the rest of the world.

Picture a photo of this little family. He's thirty years older, but otherwise it's almost the same picture as the one of us, his wife really does look a bit like my mother, posing with her hand on his shoulder. It's rather amazing to look at and linger over, like the photo of the four of us with our parents. You scrutinize the faces, can't stop asking yourself uncomfortable questions. But you're left without an answer, in the face of the absurdity of your naive insistence. It goes without saying it's impossible to divine anything at all. There's nothing to see, because what you're looking for is not in the order of the visible.

Some aesthetic considerations

> *Writing, the way it plays on both the visible and the*
> *invisible, lights up the darkness.*
> —Bernard Noël

Must a writer who was imprisoned in Auschwitz write only about Auschwitz? Of course not. Toward the end of his life, Primo Levi wrote some exuberant stories about animals. A writer has no obligation of any kind. But when it's there, as Mary Karr has said about her dysfunctional family, it would be a shame not to make the most of it.

I always want to read about sexual abuse, and at the same time something keeps me away, forbids me from delving too deeply. I've heard other survivors talking about this simultaneous fascination and repulsion. Charlotte Pudlowski's mother, who only spoke after her father had died about having been raped by him when she was a child, has talked about how, all through her life, she read every single newspaper article about incest she could lay her hands on, inexorably drawn to the subject, and yet unable to figure out what to do with this information. It made her feel less alone. What had happened to her also happened to other people, which meant it existed. It had a name, it was a crime that the headlines called monstrous. It's a recognition that suddenly makes sense of it all, liberates something within us: Those acts, that seem disconnected from reality, that seem to belong only to silence and darkness, that seem like a strange alliance between corporeal mechanics, words, and theatrical rituals, bizarrely embedded in the rest of life, are real (they happen to other people, they happened to us), against the law, horrific. And even for someone who doesn't speak out, perhaps just knowing that elsewhere there is outrage about another person who has suffered the same thing, the same silence, might offer some relief.

I rarely buy books about it. I don't like having them around. I leaf through them in the library, on supermarket shelves, at the bookstore. There are dozens of titles, new ones published every year. I've always seen them. I remember even when I was very young, alongside books like *Christiane F.*, seeing books with broken dolls on the cover and titles like *Daddy's Girl*, and *Shattered Innocence*. I'd flick through them, like Charlotte Pudlowski's mother, to get to the description of the rape. Generally at the start of the book there'll be a hint that something is not quite right, but the actual rape doesn't usually come until about a third of the way through.

Rape is a recurrent theme in literature. On top of memoir, there are hybrid works, fiction inspired by real life events, novels. Heather Lewis. Dorothy Allison. Kathy Acker. Christine Angot. Children are sexually abused in books by Émile Zola, Guy de Maupassant, the Comte de Lautréamont, Maya Angelou, Alice Walker, Toni Morrison, William Faulkner, Mario Vargas Llosa, Gabriel García Márquez, Louis-Ferdinand Céline, J. M. G. Le Clézio, David Foster Wallace.

I'd read these passages with a mixture of composure and confusion, it was upsetting and yet somehow I had to. Once I closed the book it was as if I'd done something small but worthwhile that left me feeling satisfied. Worthwhile in what way? I'm not sure I know.

It was on a Saturday afternoon, in the thin light of spring, he staggered home reeling drunk and saw his daughter in the kitchen. She was washing dishes.

A scene of everyday life. He looks at her. She's eleven years old. He feels confused. Affectionate. She's his daughter. She reminds him of his wife when they first knew each other. She has her body, her gestures, her fragility. There's something repellent about this fragility. It reminds him of his culpability, making her grow up in poverty, not being able to give her a better life. It drives him mad, she's living proof of his failure. It drives him mad that she loves him and he hates himself. She scratches the back of her leg with her toe, without stopping scraping the pans, unaware that he's standing behind her. The movement fills him with emotion, he remembers one time when he was a young man, his wife scratching her leg just like that, him kissing her calf. He falls to his knees and catches the girl's foot. She loses her balance. He does too. He loses his balance in all senses of the word, he loses himself completely.

Surrounding all of this lust was a border of politeness. He wanted to fuck her—tenderly. But the tenderness would not hold. The tightness of her vagina was more than he could bear. His soul seemed to slip down to his guts and fly out into her, and the gigantic thrust he made into her then provoked the only sound she made—a hollow suck of air in the back of her throat. Like the rapid loss of air from a circus balloon. Following the disintegration— the falling away—of sexual desire, he was conscious of her wet, soapy hands on his wrists, the fingers clenching, but whether her grip was from a hopeless but stubborn struggle to be free, or from some other emotion, he could not tell.

—Toni Morrison, *The Bluest Eye*

When I realize what's about to happen my heart quickens, I know it's coming. There's no way out. And then it happens, as if in a mist, another world. Afterward, my feelings subside. It's happened. That's it. I keep reading and the book draws me in (or maybe it hasn't got much else to say, in which case I put it back on the shelf and go off to do some shopping). I feel a kind of jubilation that I've made it through a moment in the book that I think I probably understand better than anyone, maybe even better than the author herself. I feel like I have the key to understanding the book, the world.

Reading it there's an echo of the trauma, albeit on a smaller scale and in a more detached and harmless way. You put the book back on the shelf and you're okay. It's a small joy, but a joy nonetheless: the small joy of the survivor, a bit brave but there's also a slight feeling of shame that stems from the ambiguous privilege of knowing what it means to be raped.

The most inventive of these books are constructed to be experienced as an assault, perhaps to make the reader imagine what the victim experiences, not just in the fact of telling the reader, but in the way it is told. The reader is plunged into a minutely detailed scene of abuse that goes on for pages. You can feel it on your skin, you're trapped, the language is vile, the sentences designed to make the reader feel defiled. You finish it feeling exhausted and, yes, defiled.

It's difficult to make something beautiful out of a thing like this, or to find strength in it, or to make it into a springboard to something else. It's difficult to make anything out of it at all.

There was one particular review of Margaux Fragoso's memoir, in *The Guardian*, that put me off reading it: Lólita *it isn't. With all its explicit sex, melodramatic conversations and dogged chronological detail,* Tiger, Tiger *is as dreary a read as soft porn.*

It is indeed a grueling and difficult read. The reader is a powerless witness to the enslavement of an unloved little girl who gives in to the demands of her molester and even takes pity on him. Yet oddly it's not this unbearable reality that Jenny Diski focuses on. What bothers her, what makes the book *dreary*, is the explicit sex. The writer would have done better, like Nabokov's Humbert Humbert, to protect herself by ellipsis, avoidance, metaphor, style. *But really,* as Nabokov's literary pervert assures us, *these are irrelevant matters; I am not concerned with so-called "sex" at all. Anybody can imagine those elements of animality. A greater endeavor lures me on: to fix once for all the perilous magic of nymphets.*

It's the same reason people want to ban *The Bluest Eye* from school libraries: the explicit description of the rape.

Isn't this refusal to allude to the raw, vicious reality simply a strategy of avoidance? As long as these acts are not described in detail, everything remains in a kind of blurry space that allows the reader—or the writer, or the molester, or anyone—to bolster their denial. As long as you don't see the penis of the forty-year-old man in the little girl's mouth, her eyes wet with tears from the feeling of choking, it is still possible to argue that it's about love, an insane love affair, a tale of tact and style.

During the trial my stepfather found it slightly obscene that he kept being asked to return to the concrete details of what he did to me. It exasperated him. "How many times? I don't know, sometimes it was every day, other times a month would go by without me touching her." He thought it was quite beside the point to ask him to describe the acts, or to recall how old I was at the time of the first penetration. He had more interesting things to say, for his character was complex and deep, and he had experienced an extraordinary love whose subtleties he could reveal for those prepared to make the effort to understand.

I was taught that a great work of literature goes beyond ordinary experience, transcends the individual story by becoming a work of art forged in literary language. In the words of Deleuze, a great writer *creates out of his own language one that is foreign, that does not yet exist*. By the magic of this process, the factual origin of what is being described no longer matters. It must always be about the language, for this language shields us from tears, from the ugliness of wretched flesh, from the shame of imposing the sight of autobiographical abjection on others. That's what Christine Angot means when she rejects the idea of writing "crappy memoir." What she creates is not that (it's better), it is literature. In which case it's fine to include explicit sex, because it is literary sex.

Again, I agree. I, too, want to write a heartbreaking work of staggering genius. It's what I've always wanted. I agree with the critics who refuse to succumb to sensationalism, sentiment, mawkish tales. I didn't go through all those years of studying to write inserts for the *Reader's Digest*.

But on the other hand, the idea of making art out of my story appalls me. The distance that protects us, me and my potential readers, from the splatters and fluids oozing out of real life, seems hypocritical, both excessive and mendacious. Because what is it, really, this famous Language? What makes one form of expression superior to another? In the end that's what it's about: a hierarchy of the way trauma is articulated, from the bottom (mainstream, gory, graphic, maudlin) to the top (fine writing that overturns the ordinary linguistic register to arrive at a new form of utterance), by way of the average (neither well nor badly written, repetitive, "could do better"). Why should life writing necessarily be inferior? Is it the victim who is inferior? Their life? Is it the honesty of the narrator that renders their account a lesser text? Or is it all of that at once?

To place myself in a position of superiority, to try to attain it by constructing a linguistic machine, by toppling structures, creating something new and thrilling to delight discerning critics and put myself out of reach of the ordinary reader, no longer writing about my life but writing literature—how to explain how uncomfortable this makes me feel? That is the angle I should choose. To consider life writing a kind of subgenre of literature is pure cultural elitism; but then again why not practice a touch of cultural elitism if it offers you some protection? I can't avoid the sense that there's something morally abhorrent about using suffering, torture, and despair to produce an esthetically valuable artifact. Especially if you're not making anything up, if you're exploiting the suffering of real people. The necessary condition of Nabokov's novel being admired is that he himself was not a pedophile. I think everyone would agree that if he'd written a novel about his own experience, obscured with pseudonyms, style and a certain amount of embellishment, that would be more than a little problematic. Would *Lolita* have the same literary value if it were a true story about the author and a little girl he once knew and molested?

Is creating beauty out of horror not simply creating horror? If that is the case, you cannot have one without the other. Aestheticizing violence, making the reader a hostage to terror, seems to me to be an artistic error. Not a crime, but an option unworthy of a true samurai. Not as serious as messing it up (writing a mawkish book about victimhood whose shame would haunt you forever) but not exactly desirable.

By turning my back on the safe space of fiction, I'm worried that the only thing that will happen to me with this book is I'll be invited onto radio programs about sexual abuse and be asked to summarize what I said in even simpler language than that of the book, so that distracted and jaded listeners won't have to bother to read it.

So what is appropriate then? Nothing, that's the problem. I haven't found a solution for how to talk about it. The best thing would be not to talk about it at all, not here, not in this way or in any other way, and if someone does talk about it, for that person not to be me.

My model here is Claude Ponti, who was raped by his grandfather when he was a little boy. He became an artist and author of beautiful books for children, in which he creates a whole world of his own that has nothing to do with any of that. Not exactly nothing to do with it, when you know, but a parallel universe where the young reader can confront monsters without fear, have adventures where they always end up victorious and even stronger than before. His imaginary world is a response to all the cruelty out there, a place where you learn not to be afraid of your fear. He makes no direct reference to abuse or rape. Only once he'd attained a certain level of fame, had become known for his work as an artist and for the stories and characters he created, did he begin to talk about what he had gone through, denouncing it with strength and courage, and also a kind of detachment. There's nothing to be done about it now. He has no desire to criticize his mother, who did nothing to protect him, who used to send him to stay with family and didn't see him for months on end, who sent him to live with his grandfather the rapist; who abandoned him. He describes what it's like to be *constant prey*, living in the house of a man who might molest you at any moment, in interviews ranging from this abuse to the choice of color or black and white in his illustrations.

I heard him once on the radio, responding to a journalist who asked him if the violence he had endured as a child had left any trace. Of course, he said quietly, sounding a little taken aback at being asked such a question, as if it wasn't obvious, and then he described how for years he was unable to run. The sound of his breathing when he ran or made any kind of physical effort reminded him of the sound his grandfather used to make when he was on top of him, and he would faint outright; the memory was so unbearable that his brain disconnected. I remember his lovely, gentle voice overlaid by the pulse thudding in my ears. There was silence after he spoke, the journalist must have been as thrown as I was, then he managed to bounce back with another question.

Ponti is not a survivor who makes books. He is a great author-illustrator who had an awful childhood. Like Blaise Cendrars, who is not a one-armed poet, but a poet with one arm. And the difference matters. The difference is everything.

It's not that I want to write in this autobiographical form. I'd love to be able to escape the first-person singular, to hide in some sort of plural. Not to have this disagreeable sense of telling my life story.

Oh, here they come again, these insidious judgments on their little velvet feet, like cunning wolves of doubt. Is it obligatory for autobiography to always reference the intimate, private sphere? This is an important question when it comes to this topic in particular. Making this kind of trauma a strictly personal affair becomes one more strategy of oppression because it keeps it from being discussed openly.

We don't dare ask rape victims to talk, we don't like to question them about it, we avoid bringing up the subject, it's a private matter for those who have been through it, their families and friends, it's personal, their own business. It's always been like that, we have expressions for it that have passed into everyday language: *Don't wash your dirty linen in public*. Stay silent about these terrible things, abuse, coercion, incest.

A public trial in a case of child rape seems indecent for exactly this reason. I understood this the moment I saw all those unfamiliar faces in the courtroom. And yet, when you think about the extent of intrafamilial violence, you have to wonder what the notion of privacy means when we're talking about a systemic crime committed in secret in hundreds of thousands of families. This dirty linen, this disgrace, is not mine, it is ours, it belongs to us all.

There is a poem by Jacques Prévert, "La Lessive," about parents laundering their dirty linen, they drown the daughter, who has tarnished the family's honor, in soapy water.

And the father cries
Let none of this leave this room.
We shall keep it between us
Says the mother.

There's a tendency to think that inviting a victim to talk about what happened is forcing them to relive it; but there's also a kind of revictimization in the insistence that we consider accounts of sexual abuse to be a strictly private matter, of concern only to those involved. Isolating the victim, keeping them alone with what happened to them, is a common practice in a repressive regime. Making the victim believe that they are completely alone with their persecutor, that there is no group, no solidarity, no meaning, no reality. Just you and me in a basement.

and the girl is trampled
the family, barefoot,
trample her, trample her, trample her

So what if I am telling my own story in these pages? A publisher to whom I sent the manuscript, thinking he might be interested in its unconventional form, rejected it on the grounds that it wasn't a novel. He told me he'd struggle to promote it with booksellers. In his hollow rejection letter, he politely explained, without wanting to discourage me or belittle the writing, that he only publishes literature.

I'm pretty sure that the autobiographical is simply one more weapon for confronting the unthinkable, a knife to dissect the world, an aesthetic and political choice that affirms the union of form and content. It is a means, not an end, a maze of galleries so complicated one can never find one's way out. The text is at the service of thought, even if it leads ultimately to a failure of thought. Isn't this vulnerability of the narrative voice, the way it stumbles at the inability of language to describe what is, a way of exploring the inherent contradictions of language itself? Why do we think only fiction can venture into the domain of the unsayable? Writing about reality might be no more than a tool to analyze facts, but a well-honed tool cuts to the bone. And when you reach the bone, art is never far away. Autobiography limits me, obliges me to circumscribe my experience, to enclose it in its singularity, to ensure that it is never more than what it is. But it is also about ensuring that it is never less that what it is either, that it will not be reduced to nothing, returned to the silence it sprang from, so that it can be taken up by other voices, circulated, and so that the tiger, the other tiger, can finally emerge from its cage.

Is that not, after all, the purpose of literature, to get the unthinkable out there at last?

What to do with what was done to us

Childhood victims of abuse are not absent from cultural representations. There are plenty of movies, for example, featuring characters who had childhoods similar to mine. Quite an impressive array, in fact. You can be pretty sure when you're watching one of those slightly seedy police procedurals that at some moment there'll be a storyline about child abuse. It must seem easy for screenwriters to foist it onto the plot when they're looking say for a high-impact event to justify a character's killing spree, and it always has a powerful effect on the viewer. Every time I see a scene with a child sitting on a bed as the abuser closes the door behind him, I find myself momentarily unable to breathe. But the adults who grow up from being these children are never portrayed with any subtlety. There are basically two types of character: those who never get over it and become drug addicts or prostitutes or commit suicide (à la Zola); and those who never get over it and become psychopaths who either turn into violent rapists themselves, or take cruel revenge. The revenge is as spectacular and bestial as the crime suffered by the child is inconceivable and appalling. The victim as a monster of suffering, solitude and hatred. The adult resulting from monstrous childhood assault is rarely depicted as a complex figure, part of the fabric of society, carrying the burden of the unsayable with them wherever they go. And yet, remember the statistics: one in ten. That would make a huge number of psychopaths and drug addicts and prostitutes. While it's true that those who were victims do tend to lose their way in life in greater numbers than those who were not, it's equally true that most of us slip unnoticed into the crowd of human faces, our wound one among so many.

The thing that's unbearable about resilience is that all this suffering in the end just leads—if you're lucky—to being normal. Accepting what other people get to have without trying, who sometimes don't even recognize its value, comes for us at the price of a double punishment: first the suffering, and then the arduous journey to recovery. If only resilience, as in the ability to prevail, meant that we could also prevail over the normal and gain a kind of supplement to our lives. Let our hair down, become a seer or a saint. But no, most of us go about our lives incognito, and no one would ever spot the slightest sign of what happened to us.

To become like everyone else when you have lived through something unthinkable is not the sexiest of outcomes. It might even seem a bit of a failure, like being handed the role of the living dead and sticking to it faithfully without even trying to rebel. There's a particular discourse in certain segments of society, including the counterculture where I found refuge for a time, that contends that to be normal is to be a sheep, and that setting up obstacles to desire is a form of oppression. Someone with enormous lusts is someone who lives life to the full, goes beyond the limits of our policed society to sate their inexhaustible, wild, bestial thirsts, and this bestiality embodies the life force, defies taboos, is willing to burn in the fires of hell. It almost sounds glamorous put like that, if you don't have in your mind's eye concrete images of what it actually entails.

Who wouldn't choose to be the tiger rather than the lamb, the wolf rather than the dog? Sometimes I think I'd prefer to be that person, mistress of her fate, defiled but victorious, at ease with her dark side, brandishing her contradictions, her rage, her desire, instead of being me.

And yet, if I did tend toward that, toward the dominated becoming the dominator, the warrior rising up and taking vengeance with Nietzschean resilience, wouldn't I risk in turn crushing someone weaker than me? What do you have to do to raise yourself to a superior might without becoming the oppressor of another? How do you sublimate evil into kindness and not into a new evil? And how do you ensure that this kindness matters, that it fascinates as much as the dark side?

In *Tomb Song*, Mexican writer Julián Herbert draws on his life as the child of a prostitute and explores a history of oppression and marginality as his mother lies dying. There's a scene I find particularly moving that takes place at the very end, when the reader can finally relax after the narrator's grueling and arduous journey. It almost reads like a digression, but for me it's a critically important passage.

The book opens with the adult son in the hospital at his terminally sick mother's bedside, keeping vigil for the woman who dragged him when he was a child from one brothel to the next, with whom he shared a passionate, poverty-stricken, eccentric life, who is dying as she lived, a drama adulterated with sentimental songs, the sordid and the sublime in equal measure. Herbert establishes parallel narratives, the protagonist's life and the convulsive period of Mexico's history from the 1970s to the present day. A twofold journey from guilt to oblivion, from the suffering body of the mother to the social body of the motherland. Two tales of resilience superimposed onto one another, the mostly luminous present, or rather the present feeling its way toward the light, after a battle against the dark and hellish past.

Right at the end, in a brief passage, the narrator is with his three-year-old son. He describes their daily walk in a park that bears the same name as one of the brothels where his mother once worked. They take whatever path the child chooses, watch the trains go by. The narrator follows the little boy, whose childhood is so different from his own—the son of a writer, a class defector, who takes care of him, who crouches down alongside him to look at ants. To be that person today must be like having stepped through the looking glass. There is such a startling contrast between the two worlds the narrator has known. The scene might seem beside the point, and indeed it's got nothing to do with the two principal themes of Herbert's book, his experience as the son of a prostitute, and the past fifty years of Mexican history. There's both a leap through time and a qualitative leap, from the dying mother in the hospital to this epilogue. But I can't help feeling that the narrative would not be complete without this acknowledgment of the ambiguity of it all. It's about how difficult it is to reconcile these worlds. No one ever quite leaves the nightmare behind. It is always hovering just out of sight. Yet at the same time a middle-class life and a functional family is an option, a potential place of safety. And it is a desirable option, if we can manage to overcome the things that catch us up and drag us down. It's what we want for our children.

I have a home today too. I watch my daughter and her father walking on the path ahead of me, hand in hand. Now you know what I'm thinking about, what I think about all the time, what I can't help imagining.

What is it that saves us? Can literature save us? I've always found the concept of writing as therapy very dubious. The idea that telling, telling about yourself, sharing your suffering, is a path to redemption has always disturbed me. Unburdening yourself through writing or art, as if you can rid yourself of the toxin by vomiting all your ills onto others. No, I am honestly unconvinced. And yet I do think it's literature that has allowed Julián Herbert and other writers with shattered pasts to reach a place where they can be, in a certain way, freer. But in what way? For creating art out of suffering, aestheticizing violence, leads inexorably to a dead end.

Nothing has changed about why writers who don't do it for the money write: it's art, and art is meaning, and meaning is power, as David Foster Wallace wrote.

The thing that is liberating about literature is it offers us access to something greater than we are. Greater than our pain, greater than our personal experience, greater than the intensity I've talked about. Discovering literature is like gaining access to a world of extreme risk, of encounters with the enormity of life and death, but on a different plane. It can be a consolation. A form of consolation, but never enough to save a person.

I'm tempted to appropriate the words of the historian of the two world wars that have haunted me for so long—*They rape because they can*—as if they offer a valid response to the question "Why?" Why am I writing this book? Because I can. And, like for the soldiers, the answer shatters into an infinite series of fractals that lead to melancholy, but also to rage and to joy.

If you have made it this far, you will know that the hero of this book is not the rapist. How to write in his place? I can't. I suspect that a memoir written by the rapist would be more interesting than the one you're reading now (or flicking through—I'm not even sure I would pick up my own book if I saw it on display in a bookstore). But if my stepfather were to write a book, I'd be the first to read it, for sure. Our world seen through the eyes of a child rapist; yes, that's a book I would like to read.

But here the real heroine is me, me and my tribe—not grandiose heroes, maybe more antiheroes, defending our little space, what's left of our dignity. My tribe isn't especially valiant. Sometimes you'll see us break down in tears after barely managing to get out three words during a conference where we've been invited to tell our untellable stories. Sometimes you see us on television, with shadows under our eyes and puffy faces, our hands trembling, trying to stammer out four quaking sentences to a presenter who is understanding, but hungry for sordid details we don't want to give him. We give them to him anyway.

There are so many of us. So many of us. Every year hundreds of thousands of people wake up or fall asleep transformed into one of us. An army of shadows. We don't talk about it much, we get on with our lives, but that doesn't mean we think about it any less. What gives us strength isn't noisy discussions and debates and denunciations that at last allow us the upper hand over our tormentors. I know that moral superiority is not a real victory. I will never have the upper hand. There is no possible victory, apart from little things that don't change anything. Like so many others I was raped, I was defiled and betrayed at an age when all you have is trust, and yet I grew up to become an adult who has not raped or defiled or betrayed another person in return. We do everything we can to protect the children around us, pushing aside obstacles in their path. We answer, bravely, all their questions. We carefully unravel the weft of silence with our little hands, patiently untangling the most obstinate knots. And when one nettle shirt is finished, there will be another to take apart, and we will pick up the work with our scratched and blistered fingers. And again, we will weep, a torrent of tears.

The normal world and the other place

And now, one last, brief literary analysis to illustrate all this. (If there are so many references in these pages from the English-speaking world, it's not because this literature has more of a focus on violence than that of other countries. It's simply what I had to hand, from having studied English. But these spaces can be found in other places, they are everywhere.)

In "The Other Place," a story by Mary Gaitskill that appeared in *The New Yorker* in 2011, a man in his forties is telling us of his concerns about his thirteen-year-old son, who spends all his time watching gory movies and playing violent video games. He's noticed a kind of electric shock that galvanizes his son when he's watching this stuff. It's not simply that he notices, he recognizes the sensation, knows it, he felt it himself for a long time. He still feels it, but he has learned to control it.

He tells us when it began, in his early teens, how it built from a morbid fascination with extreme violence, to the day he almost committed it. A normally dysfunctional family, divorced parents, a rather selfish and shallow mother. He drank, smoked, did drugs with his friends, all against a mental backdrop of men cutting up other men with chain saws. He noticed his friends didn't pay as much attention to the violence as he did, nothing in particular seemed to happen to them when a young woman appeared on the screen being chased down a dark street by an assailant; whereas, for him, there was definitely something happening. And it's this frisson, this electricity that he senses, detects in his adolescent son.

The man is now a successful real estate agent, married to a woman he loves and with whom he has a relationship based on trust and openness. He's told her most of the stuff about his past, his macabre inclinations, and she's accepted it as being part of a stormy, unhappy youth, like hers in fact, when she'd found refuge in drugs and extreme sex (but the narrator privately thinks hers wasn't stormy in quite the same way). He tells us about his son when he was a child, the drawings of mutilated bodies, the nightmares, and the things he's tried to do to help him deal with his obsessive tendencies. The narrative about the boy is interwoven with an episode from the father's troubled youth. It's a strange blend of ever-shifting emotions, from incipient horror at what unfolded in the past (a young man with fantasies of murder gradually getting closer and closer to committing it) to the tender efforts of the same man, now a loving father, as he teaches his son to throw a ball, or cast a fishing line.

The narrator recalls how he was drawn to situations of furtiveness and ambiguity. As a teenager, he would wander around the neighborhood alone at night, peeping into peoples' windows, even watching the little girl next door in the dark as she slept, just a few centimeters from her, so close he could see her chest as it rose and fell. He was trying to locate the tipping point that would take him to this strange place, this dimension of thrill and intensity that he called *the other place.*

One day he gets hold of a gun. He hitches a lift with a woman and orders her at gunpoint to drive to an abandoned house where he's going to kill her. At first she follows his directions to the place he's chosen to put his plan into action; then suddenly she pulls over onto the hard shoulder. She refuses to cooperate, tells him that if he wants to kill her, he can do it now.

> *The normal world and the other place were turning into the same place, quick but slow, the way a car accident is quick but slow. . . . She shifted her eyes again. She looked me deep in the face.*
>
> *"Well?" she said. "Are you going to do it or not?"*
>
> *Words appeared in my head, like a sign reading "I Don't Want To."*
>
> *She leaned forward and turned on the emergency lights. "Get out of my car," she said quietly. "You're wasting my time."*

Something about the woman's composure, the way she talks to him, shunts him out of his interior world back onto solid ground, where his urge to kill evaporates and he loses all interest in the act. For the reader too, at that moment in the car, two worlds are superimposed, we are in two dimensions, shadow and light, revulsion and empathy.

The boy comes to realize that he has reached a threshold which, if crossed, will destroy his life. It's literally that, the sense of being about to do it, that tiny transition that changes everything, abruptly pulling us back from fantasy to reality. For a moment, it seems possible, inevitable even, because everything has led up to that point. Then suddenly he can't do it. He will go no further. And somehow, obscurely, he realizes in that moment that he is not the only one in the car who knows about the other place: *I realized after she was gone that she might call the police, but I felt in my gut that she would not—in the other place there are no police, and she was from the other place.*

For a long time, this woman's face looming out of the shadows continued to haunt the narrator. Now, years later, he sees it again, not only in his own visions, but also in those of his son. Now he has to go back in order to figure out how this world emerged within him. That's why he's set up this whole system of analysis he's describing to us, to try and access his son's psyche. He's looking for ways to mitigate the influence of all those aggravating factors. Encouraging physical activity to anchor him in the real, instead of the endless video games that are like the projection onto a screen of manufactured psychological fantasies. Finding things that give him self-confidence. Surrounding him with love without smothering him.

It's not about turning the page, or changing him, it can't be ignored, it will always be there, it's part of who he is. He wants to find a way to help his son tame the monster within him. And he will never give up on him.

> *Somewhere in him is the other place. It's quiet now, but I know it's there. I also know that he won't be alone with it. He won't know that I'm there with him, because we will never speak of it. But I will be there. He will not be alone with that.*

He will not be alone with that. The words make me weep. His son won't know his father is there with him as he fights this unspeakable thing that inhabits them both. But he will be there. He promises himself. He promises us, the unknown custodians of this strange confession. I think what brings me to tears is the idea of this invisible dimension that is not menace or horror but love. I too believe in the existence of this covert kindness. I practice it whenever I can, it is my silent revenge for the evil that was done to me. And I know that other people of the shadows do the same, each of us from the corner we have been given to live.

The country of shadows

For me, the other place is a neighboring country. As in fantasy literature, it's a world that touches ours, is super-imposed onto it, a kind of fourth dimension. Once you're cast into it, you can never get out; just one looming shadow and you're dragged back there, it's beyond you to resist.

I sometimes meet people who have been or are on their way to this land of darkness. I recognize them, it's something in their eyes. I think they see it in me too. It's a mute recognition, we don't say anything. We wouldn't know what to say. And there's no point. What would we say if we could?

There's this guy who lives near me. He's a former *pandillero* who's come back to live in his village. He works the land, tends his father's plot, takes the cows out to pasture. Sometimes I see him going by in a battered old green pickup, or on foot. Occasionally we find ourselves sitting opposite each other on the minibus that goes to the nearest town. He's covered in tattoos, all the way up his neck, even up to his eyes. He must be about my age. We are not from the same world. I don't know where he has been. He doesn't know where I have been. And yet, as we exchange a few polite words about the weather, I read his eyes as if I were watching fish swimming beneath the surface of a lake. And he reads me like an open book, written in a language he might not understand, but that speaks to him clearly all the same. I can't guess exactly what was done to him, or what he has had to do to forget a little of what was done to him, but I know he is the ghost of a living person who's never had a lucky break. I can't be sure, but I sense he knows that about me too. It isn't sad. It's just this strange thing we live with. We have that in common, that unspeakable thing, but it doesn't mean we can be friends or anything.

We learn how to live with the knowledge that that world is always there, that it will always be there, just out of sight.

It is a world in which victim and abuser are reunited. I think they are the same, or almost the same shadows. It's a world where it's impossible to be ignorant of evil. It's everywhere, altering the color and flavor of everything. Ignoring or forgetting it is not an option, for the more you run from it, the quicker it catches you up. But it is possible to stand back from the brink. That is the challenge: how to remain on the threshold of this world, how to keep going like tightrope walkers along the wire, facing the future. Wavering, unsteady, but not falling. Not falling. Not falling.

WORKS CITED

BOOKS

Allison, Dorothy. *Bastard Out of Carolina*. Dutton, 1992.

Angot, Christine. *Le Voyage dans l'Est*. Flammarion, 2021.

Artaud, Antonin. *Suppôts et suppliciations*. Éditions Gallimard, 2006.

Atxaga, Bernardo. *Obabakoak*. Ediciones B, 1989. Translated by Margaret Jull Costa as *Obabakoak: Stories from a Village* (Graywolf, 2010).

Blake, William. *The Complete Poems*. Penguin Classics, 1978.

Carrère, Emmanuel. *L'Adversaire*. P.O.L., 2000. Translated by Linda Coverdale as *The Adversary: A True Story of Monstrous Deception* (Metropolitan Books, 2001).

de Kerangal, Maylis. *À ce stade de la nuit*. Éditions Gallimard, 2001.

Degroote, Ludovic. *Un petit viol*. Champ Vallon, 2009.

Deleuze, Gilles. *Critique et clinique*. Éditions de Minuit, 1993. Translated by Daniel W. Smith and Michael A. Greco as *Essays Critical and Clinical* (University of Minnesota Press, 1997).

Despentes, Virginie. *King Kong théorie*. Éditions Grasset & Fasquelle, 2006. Translated by Frank Wynne as *King Kong Theory* (Fitzcarraldo Editions, 2020).

Eribon, Didier. *Retour à Reims*. Fayard, 2009.

Ernaux, Annie. *Mémoire de fille*. Éditions Gallimard. 2016. Translated by Alison L. Strayer as *A Girl's Story* (Seven Stories Press, 2020).

Gibran, Kahlil. *The Prophet*. Knopf, 1923.

Hatzfeld, Jean. *Une saison de machettes*. Éditions du Seuil, 2003. Translated by Linda Coverdale as *Machete Season: The Killers in Rwanda Speak* (Picador, 2006).

Herbert, Julián. *Canción de tumba*. Mondadori, 2011. Translated by Christina MacSweeney as *Tomb Song* (Greywolf Press, 2018).

Kouchner, Camille. *La Familia Grande*. Éditions du Seuil, 2021. Translated by Adriana Hunter as *The Familia Grande* (Other Press, 2022).

Morrison, Toni. *The Bluest Eye*. Vintage International, 2007.

Nabokov, Vladimir. *Lolita*. Penguin Classics, 2000.

Noël, Bernard. *Le Livre de l'oubli*. P.O.L., 2012.

Ortuño, Antonio. "Un trago de aceite." In *La vaga ambiciòn*. Páginas de Espuma, 2017.

Paglia, Camille. *Vamps & Tramps: New Essays*. Vintage, 1992.

Pizarnik, Alejandra. *Poesía complete*. Lumen, 2011.

Prévert, Jacques. "La Lessive." In *Paroles*. Éditions Gallimard, 1949. Originally published by *Le Point du jour* in 1946.

Rimbaud, Arthur. "Le Coeur Volé." Translated by Edmund White as "The Stolen Heart," in *Rimbaud, the Double Life of a Rebel* (Atlas, 2008).

Sapienza, Goliarda. *L'arte della gioia*. Stampa Alternativa, 1998. Translated by Anne Milano Appel as *The Art of Joy* (Farrar, Straus and Giroux, 2013).

Sartre, Jean-Paul. *Saint Genet, comédien et martyr*. In *Oeuvres complètes de Jean Genet*, vol. 1, by Jean Genet. Éditions Gallimard, 1952. Quoted in Didier Eribon, *Retour à Reims*, Fayard, 2009.

Shalamov, Varlam. *Kolyma Stories*. Translated by Donald Rayfield. NYRB Classics, 2018.

Torres, Diana J. *Pornoterrorismo*. Txalaparta, 2011. Translated to the French by Arana Hartzea López as *Pornoterrorrisme* (Gatuzain, 2012).

Wallace, David Foster. *Both Flesh and Not: Essays*. Little, Brown, 2012.

Woolf, Virginia. *Moments of Being*. Edited by Jeanne Schulkind. Harcourt Brace & Company, 1985.

ARTICLES, MAGAZINES, PERIODICALS

Beveraggi, Jean. "7 ans de calvaire pour une fillette" [A little girl's seven-year ordeal]. *Le Dauphiné liberé*, June 2000.

Dautriat, Lucien. "Neige, c'est l'adorable prénom du premier bébé né au Forest de Vars depuis 47 ans" [Neige, the adorable name of the first baby to be born in the Vars Forest for 47 years]. *Le Dauphiné liberé*, June 3, 1977.

de Foucher, Lorraine. "À l'hôpital psychiatrique de Ville-Évrard, les violeurs en thérapie" [At the Ville-Évrard psychiatric hospital, rapists in therapy]. *Le Monde*, April 17, 2021.

Diski, Jenny. "*Tiger, Tiger* by Margaux Fragoso—review." *The Guardian*, April 11, 2011.

Dussy, Dorothée. "Dorothée Dussy, anthropologue: 'Il y a tou-jours autant d'articles de loi qui profitent aux incesteurs'" ['There are still so many legal provisions that benefit those who commit incest']. Interview by Raphaëlle Leyris. *Le Monde*, September 12, 2021.

Fragoso, Margaux. *Tiger, Tiger: A Memoir*. New York: Farrar, Straus and Giroux, 2011.

Gaitskill, Mary. "The Other Place." *The New Yorker*, February 14 and 21, 2011.

Juillard, Marianne and Odile Timbart. "Les condamnations pour violences sexuelles" [Sentences for sexual violence]. *Infostat justice*, September 2018.

La Tribune républicaine du pays de Gex. "Plus de peur que de mal" [More frightened than ever in danger]. March 11, 2011.

Lawson, April Ayers. "The Trouble with Rape." *Granta*, December 5, 2018.

Le Monde. "À propos d'un procès." January 26, 1977. An open letter written (anonymously) by Gabriel Matzneff and signed by, among others, Louis Aragon, Roland Barthes, Simone de Beau-voir, Jean-Paul Sartre, Félix Guattari, Gilles Deleuze, Patrice Chéreau, Michel Leiris, Dionys Mascolo, Philippe Sollers, and André Glucksmann, reprinted in *Libération* on January 27, 1977. In May of the same year, *Le Monde* published a second open letter demanding the repeal of laws forbidding sexual relations between adults and minors, signed by the same people, and others, including Michel Foucault and Françoise Dolto, who had not signed the first letter.

Tough, Paul. "The Poverty Clinic." *The New Yorker*, March 14, 2011.

RADIO

Foucault, Michel. "The Danger of Child Sexuality." In conversation with Guy Hocquenghem and Jean Danet. *Dialogues*. Produced by Roger Pillaudin. Broadcast April 4, 1978, on France Culture. Later published in a collection of writings by Michel Foucault.

Pudlowski, Charlotte. *Ou peut-être une nuit*. A series of seven podcasts. Louie Media, September–October 2020.

FILMS

Massart, Guillaume, dir. *La Liberté*. Triptyque Films and Films de Force Majeure, 2017. Also released as *In the Open*.

Roth, Tim, dir. *The War Zone*. Film4 and Portobello Pictures, 1999.

Sciamma, Céline, dir. *Petite Maman*. Lilies Films, 2020.

MUSIC

Oldham, Will. "I See a Darkness," Track 3 on *I See a Darkness*, Palace. Domino, 1999.

CREDITS AND PERMISSIONS